Where Social Media Marketing is Headed in the Next 5 Years

The Unconventional Guide to Build your Brand and Become an Expert Influencer Using Facebook, Twitter, LinkedIn, Pinterest, Instagram and YouTube

HENRY CHAMBERS
DEBUT BESTSELLING AUTHOR

© **Copyright 2019 - All rights reserved.**

The content contained within this book may not be reproduced, duplicated or transmitted without direct written permission from the author or the publisher.

Under no circumstances will any blame or legal responsibility be held against the publisher, or author, for any damages, reparation, or monetary loss due to the information contained within this book, either directly or indirectly.

Legal Notice:
This book is copyright protected. It is only for personal use. You cannot amend, distribute, sell, use, quote or paraphrase any part, or the content within this book, without the consent of the author or publisher.

Disclaimer Notice:
Please note the information contained within this document is for educational and entertainment purposes only. All effort has been executed to present accurate, up to date, reliable, complete information. No warranties of any kind are declared or implied. Readers acknowledge that the author is not engaging in the rendering of legal, financial, medical or professional advice. The content within this book has been derived from various sources. Please consult a licensed professional before attempting any techniques outlined in this book.

By reading this document, the reader agrees that under no circumstances is the author responsible for any losses, direct or indirect, that are incurred as a result of the use of information contained within this document, including, but not limited to, errors, omissions, or inaccuracies.

Table of Contents

Introduction 1

Chapter 1 - What is Social Media Marketing and Why is it Important? 5

    Defining Social Media Marketing 5

  Importance of Social Media Marketing 6

    Increase Demand 7

    Social Selling 12

    SEO 16

    Omnichannel Campaigns 18

    Networking and Peer-to-Peer Influence 20

    Social Media Drives Value Across the Customer Lifecycle 21

Chapter 2 - Create A Winning Social Media Marketing Strategy 25

    Understand Your Audience 26

    Map Your Goals to the Customer Lifecycle 30

    Creating Content for Social Media 34

    Define Your Writing Style for Social Media 39

    Scaling Your Content for Social 40

Chapter 3 - Choosing the Right Social Media Platform 43

  Facebook 48

  Twitter 51

  LinkedIn 53

  Pinterest 54

Instagram 56

YouTube 57

Snapchat 60

Common Social Media Mistakes to Avoid 61

    Trying to be Everywhere 61

    Failing to Know Your Audience 62

    Failing to Learn from Analytics 62

    Posting Bad Content 63

    Missing Out on Messages and Mentions 63

    Forgetting to Test 63

Chapter 4 - Social Media Advertising 65

    Define Your Goals 68

    Identify Your Audience 70

    Pick the Right Social Media Platform 71

    Determining the Right Content 72

    Select Targeting Options 75

Chapter 5 - Developing a Social Media Calendar 81

    Why Use a Social Media Calendar? 82

    Conduct a Social Media Audit 84

    Setting and Identifying Your Cadence 84

    Prepare a Social Promotion Request Form 87

    Posting Frequency on Social Networks 87

    Facebook 89

    Twitter 90

    Instagram 91

    Pinterest 91

    LinkedIn 92

YouTube 92

Snapchat 93

Social Media Daily Checklist 93

Chapter 6 - How to Structure Your Social Media Team 99

Evaluate Your Current Situation 100

Creating a Social Media Governance Board 100

Determining the Governance Members 101

Create a Board Charter 101

Clarify Social Media Goals 102

Break up the Project into Stages 102

Communicating Goals and Training Staff 102

Staffing Considerations 103

Budget for New Employees 103

Strategic Goals 104

Skills Required 104

Social Media Platforms to be Used 106

Content Strategy 107

Chapter 7 - Integrating Social Media into Your Omnichannel Marketing Strategy 109

What is Omnichannel Marketing? 111

Tips to Successfully Integrate Social Media into Your Omnichannel Marketing Strategy 112

Engage in Social Listening 112

Mixing Social Media and Email Marketing 113

Centralize the Data Collected 113

Never Ignore Your Audience 114

Support In-App Purchases 115

　　Encourage Recommendations 115

**Cross-Channel Social Media Marketing with
Marketing Automation** 116

　　Increasing Engagement 117

　　Enhanced Loyalty 118

　　Align with Consumer Behavior 118

Chapter 8 - Your Social Media Technology Stack 123

　　Developing a Social Media App 123

　　　Customer/Client 123

　　　Backend 127

　　　Database 128

Social Media and Marketing Automation 128

Popular Social Media Automation Tools 130

　　　SendinBlue 130

　　　Hootsuite 131

　　　BuzzSumo 132

　　　Mention 132

　　　AgoraPulse 133

　　　SocialFlow 133

　　　Buffer 134

　　　Socedo 134

　　　Sprout Social 135

Social Media Automation Strategy 135

　　Clarify When to Automate 136

　　Find a Way of Staying Connected 139

Chapter 9 - Measuring the ROI of Your Social Media Campaigns...141

    Awareness Metrics..144

    Engagement Metrics...146

    Conversion Metrics...148

    Customer Metrics 149

Tips to Improve Your Social Media ROI 150

Final Thoughts 155

References 163

Introduction

The advent of the internet has changed the way businesses interact with their customers. Today, businesses prefer to use the internet to connect with their esteemed clients. One of the main reasons for this is the number of people who are connected through social media platforms and other websites. Social media marketing (SMM) refers to the way in which businesses use social media to reach their current and potential clients. In this regard, most of them tend to use social networks such as Facebook, Twitter, Instagram, LinkedIn, Pinterest, YouTube, etc.

There are many people who are already using these social networks. This has been one of the reasons why entrepreneurs strive to use these platforms to reach their clients. Today, there are over 4.3 billion people who actively use the internet[1]. Out of these 4.3 billion, about 3.5 billion of them are active social media users[2]. This statistic reveals that there are over 50% of the

---

[1] "• Global digital population 2019 | Statista." 18 Jul. 2019, https://www.statista.com/statistics/617136/digital-population-worldwide/. Accessed 31 Jul. 2019.

[2] "126 Amazing Social Media Statistics and Facts | Brandwatch." 13 Jun. 2019,

world's population who use social media networks. Bearing these statistics in mind, it means that businesses should take advantage of the connectivity that these social networks provide.

The best way to understand social media marketing is by acknowledging the fact that it is a type of internet marketing. Do you recall the conventional forms of marketing that businesses used to reach their customers? Before the introduction of the internet, companies had to rely on different forms of marketing such as direct mail, flyers and brochures, print ads, and door-door sales men among others. Through these marketing channels, businesses managed to market their brands and specific products to customers.

With the introduction of the internet, marketing has changed in ways that you couldn't have imagined before. It has made it easier for businesses to achieve their marketing goals without spending a lot of money. What's more, the mere fact that there are billions of people on social media shows that companies have a wider reach, therefore, marketing products and services through social media is more advantageous compared to traditional forms of marketing.

Perhaps one of the most remarkable things about social media marketing is that you don't have to be a marketing expert to use

---

https://www.brandwatch.com/blog/amazing-social-media-statistics-and-facts/. Accessed 31 Jul. 2019.

these social networks. By using this guide, you can master the art of selling your brand over the internet. Sure, there are simple activities that you will be doing on social media such as posting images, text and video. However, there are vital tips and tricks you should consider.

It is worth noting that there are tons of other businesses who are also trying to capture their audiences' attention on social media. This means that you should aim to stand out and establish a commanding social presence. So, sharing videos and text messages is not enough; you need to know how to do this in an unrivalled way possible. This stands as a solid reason why this guide should act as your best friend now that you want to establish your social media presence. Maybe you have tried marketing your business on social media but you are not impressed with the outcome. It could also be that you failed in your social media marketing attempt.

This guide will take you through the basics of social media marketing. The manual will also outline some of the most important marketing strategies that you can adopt to help you succeed in enhancing your social presence. Throughout the guide, we will help you realize that you are making the right move to market your brand on social media. Businesses are taking up the challenge and are already benefiting from Facebook, Instagram, Twitter and the likes. To gain a competitive advantage, you have to utilize the opportunity and engage over the internet.

You might be wondering whether the social platforms you chose are ideal for your business. Frankly, with the numerous social media platforms out there, it is very easy to get confused when choosing the right one for your business. Most entrepreneurs are under the assumption that marketing on social platforms only requires marketing on the main social networks such as Facebook, Instagram, and Twitter. The reality is that this is not true. The type of business you own should define the marketing strategies that you adopt. In some cases, this could mean that you use other platforms while leaving out Facebook or Snapchat. These are some of the areas that this manual will be focusing on to guarantee that you know exactly what your business needs to thrive.

Chapter 1 - What is Social Media Marketing and Why is it Important?

With the large number of businesses that are already using social media marketing, it is quite likely that you are also motivated to walk in the same direction. Maybe you have noticed that this form of internet marketing is helping businesses grow within a short period of time. Having said this, you can't deny your excitement. You want to jump in right away and create your business' social media marketing strategy. However, before getting into too much detail, it is imperative to clearly understand what social media marketing is. It is also vital that you know the benefits that this form of marketing will have on your business. With the help of this information, you will be motivated to establish your business' social presence without hesitation.

Defining Social Media Marketing

Social media marketing is a type of internet marketing whereby social networks such as Facebook, Instagram, Twitter, and LinkedIn are used to promote a business' products and services. The use of these varying platforms helps a business to enhance its brand awareness through the content that will be shared.

Marketing campaigns created on social media often focus on a number of things. First, they aim to create an online presence on varying platforms that suit a particular business. Secondly, content created should be shareable by interested parties. Content is key to winning over potential customers on the internet. Businesses, therefore, have to place a major emphasis on coming up with unique and interesting content. And third, customer feedback is an essential factor in online marketing campaigns.

When browsing through the internet, you may have noticed websites with social buttons directing you to varying social platforms. Brands that we depend on for their products and services have an online presence. This is how social media marketing helps businesses to increase their brand awareness out there. It's all about marketing products and services over the internet.

Importance of Social Media Marketing

Before using social media marketing, you might want to find out the value that it will add to your business. Undeniably, you already know that marketing your brand on these platforms will help boost your brand awareness. However, there is more that your business stands to gain. About 93% of business people using social media to market their brands claim that it helps in increasing their business exposure. 71% of them argue that it helps in developing loyal fans.[3] To guarantee that you are not confused about social media marketing and the value it adds to your business, the following are convincing reasons why you should engage in social media marketing.

Increase Demand

A major boost you will gain through the use of social media marketing is that it will help increase demand for your products and services. This stems from the fact that there are many people who use social media networks. On Facebook alone, for example, there are more than 2 billion monthly active users[4]. With the wide audience reach that these platforms provide, it is safe to assume that it increases the demand for products and services.

The way in which social media networks present your brand out there is regarded as creation of brand awareness. As a business owner, you stand a greater chance allowing your brand to be

---

[3] "• Benefits of social media marketing worldwide 2019 | Statista." https://www.statista.com/statistics/188447/influence-of-global-social-media-marketing-usage-on-businesses/. Accessed 31 Jul. 2019.

[4] "• Facebook: global daily active users 2019 | Statista." https://www.statista.com/statistics/346167/facebook-global-dau/. Accessed 31 Jul. 2019.

noticed by many people. Accordingly, this has an impact on the demand that you will be getting for your product or service.

The help of social media engagement that you will be taking advantage of will provide you the opportunity of interacting with potential clients in the market. They will garner a deeper insight about your product's use and its benefits. The brand recognition you will get will have a positive impact on its demand.

In line with the idea of increasing demand for your goods or services, you should know that customers are always searching for solutions to their problems. Most of them can't clearly explain what their problems are. This is where your marketing efforts come in. With the right form of marketing, you will help your audience realize that your product/service is what they have been looking for.

Your marketing creativity will be required to convince customers that your product is better than other similar products in the market. Customers tend to purchase things from brands that they have tried before. This means that it might be challenging to win them over. Your social media marketing strategies will have a profound impact on the response that you will get from your audience.

To ensure that you spark interest in your audience, the following are creative social media marketing techniques that you should implement.

Product Scarcity

Many brands will want to give you the impression that their stock is limited and therefore, you should use their product before their offer ends. On many occasions, this is a strategy that will create the fear of missing out in most potential clients. As such, most of them will rush to buy your products or share information about your brand. By creating a sense of urgency in your marketing campaign, you encourage interest among your audience. Ultimately, there will be a potential increase in demand for your product/service.

Information Scarcity

Another great idea to stimulate interest around your product on social media is by sharing just enough info that your audience requires. We have seen this as customers. Oftentimes, when manufacturers are about to launch new smartphones to the market, they will create hype around their products by releasing scarce information. This creates suspense around the product and people will be anxious to purchase the product right after its launch.

The same case applies to movies and series that we often watch. Before the release of these films or shows, people are usually given a sneak preview of what they should expect. This keeps people engaged and waiting for the release of such products. So, it is always a brilliant idea to understand what your audience requires and tip them off on how your brand will meet their demand. Eventually, there is a high possibility that the demand for your product will increase.

Leveraging User-Generated Content

A good number of people will be motivated to stick to a particular brand because their friends are using it. Frankly, this is how most people shop over the internet. They only turn to products or services which have been proven and tested to be reliable. Bearing this in mind, it is worth exploiting the advantage that social media marketing offers with regard to leveraging user-generated content. This means that you could post content showing what other users are saying about your brand.

You could post images, videos, or just text detailing reviews on your product on social media. The benefit gained here is that you can easily convince your audience that your product is worth trying. What's more, this is an inexpensive form of social media marketing.

Paying Attention to the Biggest Problem

Social media marketing can also boost the demand for your product/service if you pay attention to what your customers consider as their biggest problem. This is a common marketing technique used on YouTube to gain attention. In product videos, you will come across marketers explaining to you some of the common problems that people have either when using particular products or when trying to solve their everyday issues. Their promotional message is then followed by catchy phrases that show they can offer you a solution to what you are looking for. Does this sound familiar to you? This is a social media marketing strategy that often works to boost the demand for a product.

Working with Influencers

Influencer marketing is a powerful marketing trend that has made headlines over the past few years. More and more businesses are coming to the realization that influencer marketing is indeed powerful and worth harnessing. What is influencer marketing? This is a digital marketing technique where brands use renowned people to influence others to use their products.[5] In essence, an influencer will help sway other people to rely on your brand as their ideal choice.

Working with influencers on your social media marketing campaign can make a huge difference to your marketing efforts. Influencers have a large following. Choosing the right people who are most apposite to your brand is imperative. For instance, a famous sports fan with a huge Twitter following could help you reach people who are likely to be interested in sportswear. The

---

[5] "What Is Influencer Marketing And How Can Marketers Use It ... - Forbes." 14 Nov. 2017, https://www.forbes.com/sites/forbescommunicationscouncil/2017/11/14/what-is-influencer-marketing-and-how-can-marketers-use-it-effectively/. Accessed 31 Jul. 2019.

best part is that influencers are highly influential. Thus, there is a good chance that the demand for your product will increase.

Social Selling

When businesses use social media networks to identify new prospects and interact with their clients by sharing valuable information about their brands, they are engaging in social selling. It is through this form of interaction that businesses end up developing meaningful relationships with their customers while luring new clients their way. The effect of this is that prospects and customers will likely opt for your business or brand each time they want to purchase something that you offer.

It is also worth noting that social selling doesn't entail nagging people with promotional messages. In the digital world, this is referred to as "spam". This doesn't count as social selling since you are bothering people with messages that they don't want to receive. Social selling is centered around listening to what people are saying and joining in on the conversation. When engaging in social media marketing, you should never forget the "social" aspect of it. People are using these social communities for a good reason. As such, you ought to understand how to interact with these individuals without coming off as too salesy.

There are various reasons why your business should take advantage of social selling.

Building Better Relationships

With the social tools that you will be using to listen to people's conversations over social platforms, your sales personnel can easily identify what people are saying about your business, your rivals, and the industry as a whole. With this information on hand, they can formulate ideal strategies for reaching out with meaningful information. This means that you will be providing people with what they need while at the same time gaining insights about your industry.

Better yet, you will develop strong networks with the right people who can help you boost your engagement with relevant audiences. Through this, your business instigates trust and a good business image in the minds of your audience.

Most People Practice Social Buying

Did you know that about 48% of Americans have at one point interacted with brands on social media?[6] Buying products and services over the internet is a common thing in today's digitized environment. Some individuals will opt to shop over the internet because of convenience. Others prefer shopping online due to the competitive prices offered by online companies. Before people

---

[6] "77 Online Shopping Statistics for 2019 | HostingFacts.com." 29 Jan. 2019, https://hostingfacts.com/online-shopping-statistics/. Accessed 31 Jul. 2019.

shop online, they engage with brands on their social pages. This is a purchase process that most people will not fail to consider. Besides asking questions about the product/service, people also look to know more about a brand or company.

There are instances where shoppers are discouraged from buying a specific product because of the poor communication they experience online. This leads to missed sales. The mere fact that most people are actively engaged in social buying means that your business should also practice social selling. Accordingly, your sales team should always be available to respond to prospects and customers. They should build a good rapport with the audience by knowing how best to connect with them.

Your Rivals are Using Social Selling

Your business should also consider engaging in social selling simply because your rivals are already using it. There are over 60 million businesses who have a Facebook business page. Additionally, approximately 4 million businesses actively promote their brands on Facebook.[7] Such statistics prove the fact

---

[7] "Facebook: 60 million businesses have Pages, 4 million actively ...." 27 Sep. 2016, https://venturebeat.com/2016/09/27/facebook-60-million-businesses-have-pages-4-million-actively-advertise/. Accessed 31 Jul. 2019.

that you will only gain competitive edge over your rivals in the market if you practice social selling.

Now that you understand how social media marketing can help your business through social selling, it is vital to learn a thing or two about social selling practices that can help you stand out.

- Engage Actively

Newbies in the world of social media marketing will be tempted to automate things in the hopes of saving time. Indeed, there are various automation tools that can be used for your marketing campaign. For instance, you can easily automate responses and your posts. However, this is not an ideal way of engaging with your prospects or customers.

Social media is all about being social. Therefore, people expect active engagement from you. This involves listening attentively and joining social groups which are relevant to your brand.

- Provide Value

To get the most out of social selling, you have to provide quality. People will want to follow your brand if they find value in what you post. Take note of the fact that they don't just expect product-related posts. Businesses that have many followers share engaging content which keep their audience entertained. This is the line of thinking that you should adopt when thinking about content. Additionally, time will be another crucial factor that you should mull over. Your prospects will find no value in your posts if they can't access them. This makes it important to post at the right time.

- Listen Strategically

When marketing your products and services on social media, you will gain access to information from your audience. Judging from what they will be sharing, you can get an idea of what they want. Understanding the tastes and preferences of your audience will help you serve them better. In this case, your social selling aspects will improve since you will be providing your customers with nothing but the best products and services.

SEO

Besides helping you engage productively in social selling and increasing demand for your products and services, social media marketing will also boost your SEO efforts. SEO is an acronym for search engine optimization. SEO centers around making necessary changes to your website or social media account to ensure that you are highly ranked on search engines such as Google and Bing. Optimizing your social media will ensure that you improve your brand's visibility on social media.

By regularly posting on social media, it will have an impact on your brand's awareness levels. The more you post, the more likely people will know about your company and the products/services you offer.

Social media marketing can also help your business to build an audience. Frankly, owning the best product in the market doesn't count in today's competitive environment. This is because if you fail to market your brand, no one will notice it. People will simply go for rival products as they are more visible on social media.

To become the best product in the market, you must be proactive. This means reaching out to as many people as you can. So, where are these people who might be interested in what you offer? Social media.

Facebook is ranked among the leading platforms with over 2 billion monthly active users.[8] Twitter has approximately 1.3 billion users.[9] Unquestionably, with the high number of people on these social pages, it can be a great way of reaching out to people to build an audience.

Social shares that you get from the varying social profiles that you have will also influence your search engine rankings. Have you ever wondered why there are certain companies or brands

---

[8] "Facebook: number of monthly active users ...." https://www.statista.com/statistics/264810/number-of-monthly-active-facebook-users-worldwide/. Accessed 31 Jul. 2019.

[9] "126 Amazing Social Media Statistics and Facts | Brandwatch." 13 Jun. 2019, https://www.brandwatch.com/blog/amazing-social-media-statistics-and-facts/. Accessed 31 Jul. 2019.

which are ranked better when you query a search on Google? If many people are aware of your brand's existence and its perceived importance, there is a likelihood that you will receive good rankings based on Google's algorithm. In fact, if you turn out to be the best in the market, rest assured that your brand's logo will feature on the right-hand side of the search results.

Still, it should also be noted that social media platforms are more than just social pages. Today, people have turned to these pages as search engines. Instead of querying Bing or Google, they use social platforms such as Facebook to search for information. Therefore, your search engine optimization will depend on how well you market your brand on social networks.

Omnichannel Campaigns

As more and more people get used to the internet, they try their best to avoid promotional messages. Truly, most individuals will want to avoid promotional messages that tend to interfere with their entertainment. A good example of a place where people tend to avoid these messages is on YouTube. Studies reveal the fact that 65% of online users skip video ads.[10] Interestingly, most

---

[10] "Sixty-five percent of people skip online video ads. Here's what to do." 16 Feb. 2017, https://www.cnbc.com/2017/02/16/sixty-five-percent-of-people-skip-online-video-ads-heres-what-to-do.html. Accessed 31 Jul. 2019.

of them skip these ads the moment they have the opportunity of doing so. Bearing this in mind, marketing over social media networks ought to be done strategically. Individuals should find the messages posted on these platforms as helpful and not promotional.

Omnichannel comes in to ensure that you can easily create content which suits your audience. It provides you with the opportunity of creating personalized messages that could sway your audience to rely on your brand. With the help of a good omnichannel marketing strategy, prospects will enjoy their marketing experience. Therefore, this is of great importance as it builds trust and loyalty.

Perhaps you are still trying to figure out what we mean by omnichannel marketing. Simply put, this is a sales approach which aims to consider the marketing experience of customers on different sales channels. For instance, some online shoppers will prefer to browse through their smartphones while others will opt to use their computers. In addition, there are others who will shop when they are engaging with their friends on different social media pages. You should understand that customers expect a seamless experience when transitioning from social networks to complete their purchase on your commerce website or other digital platforms.

Accordingly, social media marketing gives you the advantage of providing a smooth shopping experience to your prospects. So, besides using your business page to sell products, social media platforms are also worth utilizing.

As people enjoy the ease of shopping that you provide them, there is a certainty that sales will increase. Who doesn't love the idea of spending less than 5 minutes purchasing products? Omnichannel campaigns help assure that your clients enjoy the convenient shopping that you provide them.

Networking and Peer-to-Peer Influence

There are billions of people using social media networks today. On an individual level, people turn to social media to help them connect with other people. The worldwide connectivity that people gain also benefits businesses in many ways. Businesses can have multiple accounts on Twitter, Facebook, YouTube, Snapchat, etc. All these accounts provide business owners with the opportunity to meet people from all walks of life. Moreover, businesses can also connect with each other and provide enhanced services to their esteemed customers.

Depending on your business niche, social media not only gives you an opportunity to interact with your current customers, but you can also link up with potential clients. A single tweet can general multiple leads due to peer-to-peer influence. Individuals on social media fancy the idea of following brands that some of their friends are following. There is a sense of trust here since they trust their friends with their brand choices. This has affected us at one point when shopping. At times, we settle for products/services simply because we know friends who have used similar products or services. As such, social media gives you the benefit of networking with people while you reap the benefits of peer-to-peer influence.

Social Media Drives Value Across the Customer Lifecycle

Using social media to market your brand or company can also have a positive impact on every step of your customer's lifecycle. Once you learn how to make the best out of social media marketing, you will realize that it entails more than just marketing your products/services. It is also worth pointing out that there are varying marketing strategies which can be utilized in the different stages of any customer's life cycle. New customers will be targeted using a varying promotional strategy as compared to loyal customers. Social media marketing gives you the advantage of personalizing your marketing efforts depending on your customers' lifecycles.

Let's consider an ordinary scenario where you are using social media to market to prospective clients, repeat clients, and loyal customers.

Attracting Prospective Customers

Any business, whether large or small, will have to work on attracting potential clients to depend on their products/services.

To effectively achieve this, a solid marketing plan is required. Marketing goals here will include raising awareness of the brand as well as creating interest. To attract new clients, marketers should spend time engaging in social listening. They should strive to comprehend what their target audiences are looking for.

Influencing Repeat Customers

Once a customer has made a purchase, this should not be the end of their relationship with your business. In fact, relevant marketing efforts should be in place to guarantee that these clients depend on your products/services again. The type of content shared on social media will have a major impact on whether or not customers will depend on your brand again. Ideal content to use here should encourage conversions. A great idea here would be to post content featuring celebrities whom you use as influencers on your social media campaign.

Loyal Customers

Customers who often depend on a particular company for their products/services portray their sense of passion towards what they are getting. Oftentimes, they will choose to depend on brands that they have at once dealt with as opposed to trying new brands in the market. You can't expect loyalty if content shared is not engaging or that it is disturbing. Using the right social media marketing strategy can give a huge boost to your conversion rate. The more loyal customers depend on your brand, the more that sales will increase.

Clearly, there is a lot that your business will gain through social media marketing. One crucial factor that you should always bear in mind is that your business exists in a highly competitive environment. Therefore, if you are going to promote your products using social media, you should strive to stand out. This calls for the formulation of a working strategy which is not only unique, but that it works for your business. This area will be discussed in depth in the next chapter.

Chapter 2 - Create A Winning Social Media Marketing Strategy

Most businesses in today's world understand that they should have a social media business profile. However, their perception is that their social media pages should be managed just like any other personal account. This leaves companies granting access to junior staff members to manage the accounts since they are young and they think they should know all about social media. Unfortunately, running business social media profiles in this manner only hinders companies from benefiting from their marketing efforts.

Posting content and hoping that people will follow you is not the best of strategies to adopt in social media marketing. In fact, doing this only risks your business being exposed by rival firms in the industry. It is vital for businesses to come up with a practical strategy which will guarantee that they run their marketing campaign thoughtfully. What's more, a strategy ensures that the business' goals are approached with a sense of purpose. You know what you want to achieve and the steps to take to accomplish your set goals. This section will take you through the process of creating an ideal social media marketing strategy.

Understand Your Audience

Your first step towards creating a working social media marketing strategy is to understand who you are dealing with. Who are you targeting on social media? If you are targeting the younger population, which social media pages are they using? Are they using Facebook, Instagram, or Snapchat? Getting this information accurately warrants that you target your audience using the right platform and the best content that suits them.

It is risky to make assumptions about your audience. Maybe you want to assume that since you are targeting the young population most of them are on Facebook. Making such assumptions will only mislead you. In the end, you might end up sharing your promotional content to the wrong audience. This will be the end of the road for you as your marketing efforts will not pay off.

Start by doing your homework thoroughly. Research how different demographic groups are using social media pages. The following chart depicts this information.

Figure 1:

Use of different online platforms by demographic groups

Use of different online platforms by demographic groups
% of U.S. adults who say they use ...

	Facebook	YouTube	Pinterest	Instagram	Snapchat	LinkedIn	Twitter	WhatsApp
Total	68%	73%	29%	35%	27%	25%	24%	22%
Men	62	75	16	30	23	25	23	20
Women	74	72	41	39	31	25	24	24
White	67	71	32	32	24	26	24	14
Black	70	76	23	43	36	28	26	21
Hispanic	73	78	23	38	31	13	20	49
Ages 18-29	81	91	34	64	68	29	40	27
18-24	80	94	31	71	78	25	45	25
25-29	82	88	39	54	54	34	33	31
30-49	78	85	34	40	26	33	27	32
50-64	65	68	26	21	10	24	19	17
65+	41	40	16	10	3	9	8	6
<$30,000	66	68	20	30	23	13	20	20
$30,000-$49,999	74	78	32	42	33	20	21	19
$50,000-$74,999	70	77	34	32	26	24	26	21
$75,000+	75	84	39	42	30	45	32	25
High school or less	60	65	18	29	24	9	18	20
Some college	71	74	32	36	31	22	25	18
College+	77	85	40	42	26	50	32	29
Urban	75	80	29	42	32	30	29	28
Suburban	67	74	31	34	26	27	23	19
Rural	58	59	28	25	18	13	17	9

Note: Whites and blacks include only non-Hispanics. Hispanics are of any race.
Source: Survey conducted Jan. 3-10, 2018
"Social Media Use in 2018"

PEW RESEARCH CENTER

Source: "Use of different online platforms by demographic groups - Pew Internet."[11]

---

[11] "Use of different online platforms by demographic groups - Pew Internet." https://www.pewinternet.org/2018/03/01/social-media-use-

In regard to the above graphical information, if you are going to target college students, it means that an ideal platform that should use in your marketing strategy is YouTube. This is because the data above shows that 85% of college students use YouTube while 77% of them use Facebook. Only 32% of them use Twitter and 26% use Snapchat. With the help of the information detailed in the figure above, you can make sound decisions on which platforms to best target your audience.

Further analysis should be done to determine all relevant information about your audience. You shouldn't forget to consider the times when they often use social media and find out the frequencies of their social media use. For instance, more Facebook users visit the platform daily compared to other platforms such as YouTube, Instagram and Snapchat. This information is as portrayed in the figure below.

---

in-2018/pi_2018-03-01_social-media_a-01/. Accessed 1 Aug. 2019.

Figure 2:

Source: "Social Media Use 2018: Demographics and ...."[12]

Evidently, knowing your audience gives you an upper hand as you will know the best strategy to approach them. Thus, it is crucial that you carry out in-depth research about your audience before doing anything else.

---

[12] "Social Media Use 2018: Demographics and ...." 1 Mar. 2018, https://www.pewinternet.org/2018/03/01/social-media-use-in-2018/. Accessed 1 Aug. 2019.

Map Your Goals to the Customer Lifecycle

Next, you should think about the purpose of your social media use. Why do you want to use social media to promote your products and services? Numerous businesses create their social media business profiles simply because their rivals are doing the same. Marketing on social media without any particular goal will only affect the performance of your business. This is because you won't know exactly why social media marketing suits your business.

It is imperative that your goals should be in line with the customer's lifecycle. The journey of your customer begins with awareness about the product/service you are offering and ends with customer advocacy. Throughout the varying customer journey stages, you should have clear goals on how you will approach your customer.

Awareness

The first step you will take in your marketing campaign is to create awareness about your brand. Your brand will not benefit at all if people don't know about it. So, your marketing campaign efforts should aim to ensure that your target audience notices your brand in the market. Some of your goals here will entail:

- Name Recall

You want people to put your brand ahead of others when questioned about certain products or services. If they remember your brand, then you will have accomplished the name recall goal.

- Recognition

In addition, part of creating awareness requires that customers should be able to identify your brand and differentiate it from your industry rivals. Your target market should be able to identify your company or brand by simply looking at your logo. The adverts you feature should also distinguish you from other companies. Accomplishing the goal of brand recognition is very important as it prevents your audience from confusing you with your market rivals.

Engagement

Social media engagement is a catalyst for your brand's growth on social media. The right form of engagement can give a huge boost to brand awareness. Eventually, this will pave the way for increased conversion rates. Think about engagement like a dinner party that you are hosting. Your role here is to welcome people and encourage them to feel at home.

The goals that you will be setting for yourself here will be to increase the number of likes, shares, follows, and retweets, etc. This will show that you are indeed increasing the rate at which you are interacting with your target audience. Engagement is all about ensuring that the social aspect of social media is homed in on. This way, you end up creating meaningful relationships with your target market.

Your prospects and current customers don't want to feel as though they are interacting with robots. Therefore, your goal should be to humanize your brand on social media. Let your followers have the feeling that they are communicating with people. Your social media engagement goal should strive to make this possible.

Some of the goals that you should aim to accomplish could take the form of:

- Getting feedback concerning marketing campaigns and specific products
- Changing people's perceptions about your brand
- Provide relevant information to make it easy for clients to make the final purchase
- Finding leads

Purchase

Of course, when engagement is done well, there is certainty that customers will want to depend on your brand. This means that they will make their first purchase. Your marketing efforts on social media should not just stop there. It is imperative that you consider any future plans to contact the customers about any existing product offers that they would like to take advantage of.

Accordingly, your goal here will be to acquire the customer's contact information.

Similarly, your campaign should find out whether the customer is satisfied with the level of services they received. This calls for a survey. Use this opportunity to ask them to offer suggestions on how your company can improve its level of service provision. Moreover, you can also ask about the difficulties they experienced while shopping for products online. The point here is that you need to develop a solid relationship with the customers that make a first purchase. Keeping the customers engaged gives them the perception that your brand values them.

Retention/Loyalty

Your level of customer retention will depend greatly on the quality of content that you share. If you share nagging content, expect clients to mark your promotional messages as spam. Sharing relevant content is therefore crucial towards customer retention on social media. Efforts towards retaining your customers should include using the feedback you obtained from them and making necessary changes to meet their demands. Give your followers the feeling of being part of the process by showing them that you changed your service provisions or product by listening to their suggestions. Eventually, this leads to increased customer satisfaction.

Advocacy

Customers who are happy with the products/services that you offer will not hesitate from recommending your brand to other people. You want your customers to act as brand ambassadors and advocate your brand over rival brands in the industry. This requires that you motivate your loyal customers to share information about your product/service. This is where call to action messages come in. Your promotional messages should constantly remind people about the value of sharing promotional messages to their social circles. This is the same way in which we often share videos that we like on YouTube.

Creating Content for Social Media

Once you understand your audience and you have created SMART goals on how you will be targeting your customer in the stages of their lifecycle, the next thing to do is to plan your content. Of course, you can't just post to each and every social media page that comes to mind and expect the best results. You have to come up with a social media content strategy which will define how you will conduct the process.

In the process of creating content on social media, you should strive to understand the factors that motivate people to share content. There are several factors which encourage people to share information that is posted on social networks. Some people will choose to share content for the sake of seeking approval from their social circles. In a way, they aim to express their personalities through the content they post. Others share content because they love to communicate. Digital communication gives people the advantage of communicating with others by simply using their handheld devices. We cannot forget the fact that social media can also be used as a great platform to support ideas. More importantly, these platforms entertain people. There are numerous memes, music, videos, and text messages which are posted to entertain.

The process of creating quality content on social media can be overwhelming since there is a lot to mull over. Nonetheless, below are significant tips which will make sure you end up creating shareable content.

Have Your Audience in Mind

Your target audience will want to be exposed to content that is helpful to them. Sharing content that is only related to your brand might appear desirable, but this will only be considered uninteresting to your audience. Put yourself in the shoes of your audience, what would you want to see on a Facebook or Twitter post? Certainly, if you are looking to entertain yourself, you will want to see funny videos. Alternatively, you might also want to read about something helpful that you might have been having a problem dealing with.

Marketers should have their audience in mind when crafting their messages on social media. This is the best way you will come up with highly engaging content. Why? Because your followers will feel that what you share resonates with them.

Consumer-Generated Content

Another great idea to incorporate when coming up with social media content is to use ideas from your customers. The advantage gained here is that you will never run out of ideas when trying to be creative. It is easy to pick up ideas from what your customers are saying on social media. Say your audience finds a particular video funny and that the information is trending. You can utilize this opportunity to center your promotional message around the video. This will leave your followers entertained and they will be encouraged to share the content in their social circles.

Focus on Daily Updates

For optimal marketing results, you ought to make sure that your posts are always fresh and relevant. This calls for regular posting. Consistent posting and updating content on a daily basis increases the likelihood of your content to be seen by your target market. Whilst doing this, you should not forget the fact that timing is key to making your content visible amongst your audience. As such, do not just post because you feel like it. Instead, consider times when your customers are online on different social media platforms.

Create Infographics

If you really want to capture your audience's attention from the word 'go', then you ought to consider using infographics. Studies reveal that content with images get more likes and views. This makes it a viable option for reaching a wide audience. Moreover, content with images increases the likelihood of your information being shared by people.[13]

Offer Incentives

Additionally, you should mull over the fact that people love freebies and other incentives. This is a great technique of generating interest around your products/services. You can easily encourage your followers to like or share a particular page so that they can be rewarded with the incentives you are offering.

Use Video Content

Over the past few years, the use of video marketing has been on the rise. In the United States alone, 85% of internet users

---

[13] "85 Content Marketing Statistics To Make You A ... - OptinMonster." 7 Jan. 2019, https://optinmonster.com/content-marketing-statistics/. Accessed 1 Aug. 2019.

watched videos online on a monthly basis.[14] This shows that you stand a good chance of reaching a wider audience if you use video content.

Use a Consistent Schedule

An integral part of your content creation process should consider posting content at the right time. Posting consistently guarantees that your target market is always engaged. There are different times that you should consider when posting on the social platforms that you have a business profile on. If you will be using Facebook, the best times to post will be from Wednesday to Sunday, mostly in the afternoon. As for Twitter, posting on weekdays either in the afternoon or in the evening is recommended. Content should be posted on Instagram from Monday to Friday as early as 2 a.m. or late in the afternoon at 5 p.m.[15]

---

[14] "10 Video Marketing Statistics for 2019 [Infographic] - Oberlo." 23 Mar. 2019, https://www.oberlo.com/blog/video-marketing-statistics. Accessed 1 Aug. 2019.

[15] "Your Must-Have Social Media Content Strategy | Sprout Social." 29 Nov. 2017, https://sproutsocial.com/insights/social-media-content-strategy/. Accessed 1 Aug. 2019.

Define Your Writing Style for Social Media

You must be wondering "why style?" When questioned about style out of the context of what we are talking about, you might think about fashion. Style defines our personalities in profound ways. What you choose to wear can send a message about the type of person you are. The same case applies to communication. Your communication style will say a lot about you.

In marketing, your communication style will have an impact on the emotional appeal you will be creating in the minds of your audience. As such, this will also influence the decisions they will make. Your writing style will play a vital role in regard to winning your audience's trust. Using inappropriate language when creating content will only push your followers to reject a message you are posting. On the contrary, the right style will prove to them that you not only respect them but you also "get" them. Therefore, an ideal writing style will lower the likelihood of your audience resisting your marketing efforts.

Similarly, your writing style will also help build you an identity in the marketing world. We've all gone through certain content that we find joy in reading. As a marketer, you should develop a creative writing style that inspires action from your followers. You are looking to encourage them to change their perceptions about your brand and make the final purchase. For that reason, an appropriate writing style should make this a reality.

It is also worth pointing out that your writing style will impact how your message will be decoded by your targeted receivers. This means that you should use the right communication style which will ensure that your message is understood and received positively.

Scaling Your Content for Social

Engaging in well-planned content marketing will ensure that you reach your audience with the right promotional messages. Eventually, this transforms into more views, likes, follows, and retweets. Nonetheless, you might want to question yourself about the direction that your business will take during its peak performance. In this regard, it calls for an adjustment of your marketing strategy. Making changes here and there warrants that you can continue benefiting from your marketing efforts and help your business to grow. When faced with such a dilemma, the best move to take is to scale your content.

Scaling your content refers to your company's ability to grow past its optimal performance and continue experiencing growth. Besides increasing the number of posts on social media, you should also be mindful of the quality of content you post. To achieve this feat, the first step that you will have to take is to create a comprehensive content marketing strategy. In addition, increasing your spending on content marketing will also be required. Not to mention, you will also have to contemplate on whether you should hire specialized writers or not. Hiring experienced personnel guarantees that content can be produced efficiently.

Without question, the information detailed herein signals to you that there is a lot you need to consider when creating a social media marketing strategy. You have to plan for the entire process right from the beginning to the end. At the onset of your campaign, you should come up with realistic goals which will guide you in all stages of your customer's lifecycle. Likewise, you will have to do your homework in the early stages of your campaign to ensure that you understand your audience. All the tips which have been discussed in this section should help you in creating a social media strategy that will guide you towards success.

Chapter 3 - Choosing the Right Social Media Platform

Running a successful business over the internet is time-consuming. Entrepreneurs struggle to find time to check all the social media pages they are active on. Narrowing down to a few social media pages could also cause a problem since you are not certain which social media pages are worth using in your campaign. Undeniably, most newbies are confused about which social networks they should incorporate in their marketing strategy. This leaves most of them going for popular social pages such as Twitter, Facebook, Instagram, and YouTube.

While it might seem like a good idea to rely on top rated social networks, it is not always the case considering the fact that social media channels are not all similar. Some platforms are only used by certain types of users. For instance, Pinterest is used by more women than men. Taking this into consideration, you will opt to use Pinterest if you are targeting women to use your products/services.

Before looking into the varying social media pages, let's take a look at important tips that should help you settle for the best social channel.

Consider Your Customers

When using social media to promote your business, it is highly recommended that you strive to understand who your target market is. In line with this, you have to do research on your customers and find out what social media pages they are using. The age bracket of your audience matters a lot. For the younger population, your best bet will be to use Instagram and Snapchat. These platforms are popular among people aged 18-24 as shown in the figure below.

Figure 3:

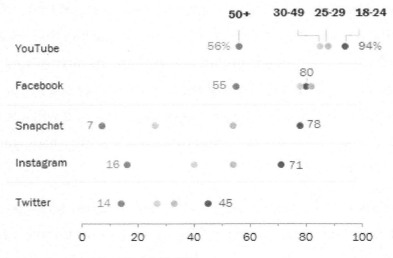

Source: "Social Media Use 2018 - Pew Internet."[16]

Other demographic factors that should be kept in mind include income, education, location, and gender. These factors will tell you a lot about who your customers are. Your research should reveal to you that there are more women than men who use Facebook in the United States. In addition, there are a higher number of college students who use Instagram compared to LinkedIn.[17] Such statistics give you a clear analysis of the social networks that would be greatly important to reach your audience.

Do You Have Time?

Furthermore, you also have to think about the time that you have to manage your business. Sure, you might think that the best way of promoting your brand is by having an online presence on many social channels. However, this might be time-consuming and financially draining if you are still a small business. Big brands have the funds to facilitate this. They have a marketing

---

[16] "Social Media Use 2018 - Pew Internet." 1 Mar. 2018, https://www.pewinternet.org/2018/03/01/social-media-use-in-2018/. Accessed 2 Aug. 2019.

[17] "Social Media Fact Sheet - Pew Internet." 12 Jun. 2019, https://www.pewinternet.org/fact-sheet/social-media/. Accessed 2 Aug. 2019.

team capable of working on different social networks and ensure that things are running smoothly.

Prior to committing yourself to many social media pages, think about the size of your business. As a market entrant, you might consider focusing on a few channels where your customers are. Devoting your time to a few channels guarantees that you deliver your best and attract a huge following.

Content

The type of content you will be posting will also have an influence on the social channels that you will be using. If you are a fan of creating videos, then an ideal platform to post your content will be YouTube. If you prefer creating images, then Instagram will be your best bet. Regardless, you shouldn't be limited to one or two social media pages. Remember, there are millions of people on other social networks that would be interested in the products/services you offer. As such, ensure that you don't suffocate your marketing possibilities.

Think About Your Rivals

Where are your rivals on social media? Sometimes it can be a good idea to study your competitors as a way of understanding how to operate in a particular market. With regard to social media marketing, your competitors will tell you a lot about the best platforms to use and the marketing strategies that you should adopt.

Studying your rivals doesn't necessarily mean that you should copy them. You should be creative enough and learn from the mistakes they are making. For instance, if your competitors are not performing well on Facebook, you should take advantage of this opportunity and find a way of gaining a huge following on the platform. In other cases, it might be a red flag that tells you to avoid investing in certain channels. So, you shouldn't follow your competitors blindly, but try your best to learn from them.

Reflect on Your Social Media Marketing Goals

Don't forget to mull over the marketing goals that you have in mind. What do you expect from your marketing campaign? Your marketing goals will not only have an impact on the strategy that you will be adopting, but it will also affect the platforms you will be choosing. Some of the goals that you might have set for yourself include increasing brand awareness, community building, increasing traffic to your business website and boosting conversion rates.

Once you have considered the discussed factors, your next step will be to pick your social media channels. The following paragraphs take a closer look into each platform and detail the best content that should be posted in the respective platforms.

Facebook

About 69% of Americans use Facebook. On top of that, there are approximately 60 million businesses with active business profiles.[18] Before rushing to use Facebook as your ideal marketing platform because of these statistics, you should stop and consider how people use this channel. Often, people use this platform to connect with their friends and relatives and as a way of killing time. Most of the time you will find people quickly scrolling through shared videos and photos.

Considering this information about Facebook, you should be in a position to determine whether or not the platform is right for your business. For example, if you are not going to post short videos and simple images, then there is a high likelihood that people will ignore your promotional messages. Take note of the fact that people will only share content that they find engaging. As such, you cannot ignore this fact since it is a determining factor as to whether you will succeed in your marketing campaign or not.

---

[18] "126 Amazing Social Media Statistics and Facts | Brandwatch." 13 Jun. 2019, https://www.brandwatch.com/blog/amazing-social-media-statistics-and-facts/. Accessed 2 Aug. 2019.

Moreover, you have to think about the fact that there are over 2 billion Facebook users.[19] Sure, you might consider this a huge advantage since it gives you an opportunity to reach a wide market. Nonetheless, it creates a problem when you cannot penetrate through the noise to get your message to the intended audience.

Here are a few pointers that you should use to make sure that your marketing campaign on Facebook thrives.

Use Paid Advertising

The Facebook algorithm keeps changing and it is not surprising that paid advertising would lead to higher visibility for your brand. Assuming that you have budgeted for your Facebook marketing campaign, taking advantage of paid advertising will boost your marketing efforts. Besides increasing your reach, Facebook ads will also increase the likelihood of sharing your content to people who are interested in what you are offering. As such, this will also have an impact on the conversion rate.

Another admirable feature of Facebook ads is that a marketer can create focused promotional messages to target a particular demographic. Interestingly, you can specify the age, gender,

---

[19] "126 Amazing Social Media Statistics and Facts | Brandwatch." 13 Jun. 2019, https://www.brandwatch.com/blog/amazing-social-media-statistics-and-facts/. Accessed 2 Aug. 2019.

location, and even the device that your target marketing is using. You cannot miss out on any potential leads that you were targeting.

Go Live

Furthermore, you can also boost your reach by choosing to go live using the Facebook Live feature. Facebook users will want to tune in and be part of what you are doing. The live feature can be of great use if you are looking to boost your social media engagement.

Build a Community

What's more, you can engage on a personalized level with your fans by creating a group. Facebook groups bring together people with similar interests. Using this platform, your audience can share the experiences that they have when using your product/service. Conversations around your brand will greatly improve your SEO rankings both on Google and other social media pages.

A crucial thing to remember when posting to your Facebook groups is that you shouldn't appear too salesy. Hard selling will only push away your followers. Use these groups to inform your audience about any exclusive offers that they would want to take advantage of. Alternatively, it can be a great place to inform your audience about promotions you are conducting and any discount offers in the market.

Use Facebook Messenger

Facebook Messenger is an app that lets you communicate conveniently with people around your social circle. Businesses have also turned to this app as one of their marketing solutions. The good thing about using the mobile application is that your followers can conveniently respond without necessarily logging into their Facebook accounts.

Twitter

Most people use Twitter to keep themselves updated on what's going on in the news and for networking purposes. To attract a following to your brand, you should bear this in mind. People will retweet your tweets if they find them funny and informative.

Another crucial aspect of Twitter that you should understand is the use of hashtags. Conversations usually center around hashtags. Accordingly, the right hashtag use will have a positive influence on your audience reach. The feature can also help you find out what people are saying about the product/service that you are offering.

The real-time updates that Twitter offers to its users should be an added advantage to your business if you are planning to enhance your customer service experience. There is no doubt that people will love the prompt responses and assistance that you will be offering them. Eventually, this will build a good brand image.

Consider the following tips when using Twitter for business.

Join the Conversation

One of the biggest perks of using Twitter to promote your business is that you can join conversations without necessarily having any connection with those you are interacting with. It is not a must that people have to follow you for you to join their conversations. Why is this important for your business campaign? Joining trending conversations can be a great way to create awareness of your brand. In addition, you can utilize this opportunity to introduce your brand as a market leader by offering insightful information. When people feel that they can get value from what you are sharing, they will not hesitate to follow you.

Make Good Use of Hashtags

Sure, joining trending conversations will get the word out there about your brand. Regardless, this depends on whether you join relevant conversations. It is not a must that you join every discussion that is trending. It is crucial that you first determine whether people are talking about something that is relevant to what you are offering. This is an important factor to consider as it will have an influence on whether people find your content informative or irritating.

Experiment with Paid Advertising

Paid advertising can also work on Twitter. However, this only applies when you are sure that your followers are active on Twitter. This ascertains that your promotional message gets to the intended audience. You can advertise on Twitter by either using promoted trends, promoted accounts, or using promoted tweets.

LinkedIn

Compared to other social media pages, LinkedIn has earned a name for itself for being a platform that is mostly used by the adult population. In the United States, 27% of adults use this platform.[20] The advantage of using this channel to promote your brand is that it is less cluttered. It primarily focuses on professionals. Therefore, if you are looking to connect your business with professionals, this can be a great option.

The following are suggestions which can help you succeed when marketing your business on LinkedIn.

---

[20] "126 Amazing Social Media Statistics and Facts | Brandwatch." 13 Jun. 2019, https://www.brandwatch.com/blog/amazing-social-media-statistics-and-facts/. Accessed 2 Aug. 2019.

Prioritize the Use of Video

The power of using video content on social media marketing also applies to your marketing campaigns on LinkedIn. Video content provides you with a great way of engaging with your audience. When creating these videos, you shouldn't forget the fact that people prefer to watch short videos. For that reason, you should strive to keep your videos short and entertaining.

Build Content on the Platform

You might have the perception that you can increase your reach by posting links from other social networks to your LinkedIn business profile. While this is possible, it is not advisable. Instead of sharing links to your YouTube video on LinkedIn, you should consider uploading the videos directly to the platform. This will increase the chance of the videos being watched by your followers.

Pinterest

Estimates show that there are 200 million active monthly Pinterest users.[21] Concerning gender, there are interesting

---

[21] "126 Amazing Social Media Statistics and Facts | Brandwatch." 13 Jun. 2019, https://www.brandwatch.com/blog/amazing-social-media-statistics-and-facts/. Accessed 2 Aug. 2019.

statistics that you should mull over. This is shown in the figure below.

Figure 4:

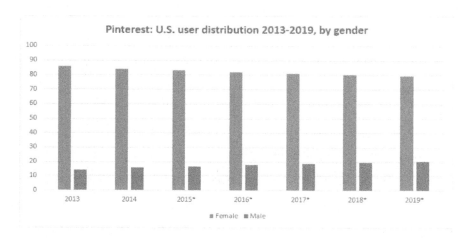

Source: "• U.S. Pinterest user distribution by gender 2019 | Statista."[22]

Using the statistics above, it is evident that females dominate the platform. Perhaps this is influenced by the type of content that is usually posted. Common pins that you will find on this platform are recipes, lifestyle, travel, fashion, and beauty. These factors should determine whether or not this is the right platform for you to post your content on.

---

[22] "• U.S. Pinterest user distribution by gender 2019 | Statista." https://www.statista.com/statistics/408229/us-pinterest-user-gender/. Accessed 2 Aug. 2019.

Instagram

Instagram is one of the leading and fastest-growing social platforms today. It has 1 billion active users who use the platform on a monthly basis.[23] Undeniably, this is a huge audience and thus, your business can attract an immense following using the platform.

Prior to using Instagram, you should take note of the fact that 64% of its users are between 18-29 years old. In addition, video posts are considered to receive more engagement compared to image posts.[24] Taking this into consideration, if you are going to engage your audience using images and videos, this is a platform that you should not forget to incorporate into your marketing strategy. Whilst doing this, you should recall that young people dominate this platform. All these demographics should be considered as they will have an effect on the response you will get from your audience.

Post More Stories

---

[23] "17 Instagram Stats Marketers Need to Know for 2019 | Sprout Social." 22 Apr. 2019, https://sproutsocial.com/insights/instagram-stats/. Accessed 2 Aug. 2019.

[24] "17 Instagram Stats Marketers Need to Know for 2019 | Sprout Social."

Just like Facebook, Instagram changes its algorithm frequently. This means that you cannot be certain that your content will reach your intended audience. Therefore, to avoid this, you should post consistently.

Use IGTV

The use of longer vertical videos is now made possible through the use of IGTV. It provides businesses with the advantage of engaging more with their audience since they can create lengthier videos.

YouTube

YouTube can also give a huge boost to your social media engagement levels. Every day, people watch over 1 billion hours of videos on the platform.[25] This shows that you can capture your audiences' attention by posting high-quality and engaging videos. Besides this, the channel gives you the opportunity of posting instructional videos about your products/services. Therefore, you can make good use of it to convey information about your product use and its benefits.

---

[25] "126 Amazing Social Media Statistics and Facts | Brandwatch." 13 Jun. 2019, https://www.brandwatch.com/blog/amazing-social-media-statistics-and-facts/. Accessed 2 Aug. 2019.

Since video is the future of social media marketing, the following pointers will guide you to ensure that you don't miss out on the opportunities that YouTube creates for businesses.

Optimize Your Videos

To get the most out of the videos you will be posting, you should optimize them. Unfortunately, most people give up on their first attempt when things fail to work out. It is worth noting that it takes time for you to gain the right traction. Therefore, you should be patient enough for this to happen. Instead of giving up, you should work on improving the quality of your videos and optimizing them.

Ideal optimization requires that you use the right keywords on your YouTube videos. Label your videos appropriately to guarantee that they can easily be found by your audience. Using the right keywords based on what your followers are looking for is highly recommended. Besides this, you should also accompany your videos with an appropriate video description. This will explain what your video is all about. Remember to add links where your followers can reach you, like on your business website as well as the social media profiles that you have.

Schedule Your Videos

Scheduling videos is another important thing to bear in mind since your followers will want to see more of your content when they are online. This means that your videos should be structured in order to engage the viewer for long periods of time. The benefit gained here is that it keeps your audience glued to your YouTube channel without getting distracted by other videos.

Optimize Your Channel

You can also increase the number of views you get on your YouTube page by optimizing your channel. This is a simple process if you focus on customizing your profile with detailed information about your business. When doing this, the use of keywords should be prioritized as this is what will bring your visitors to your channel. If you are not sure what the right keywords are to use, always study what your rivals are doing. If they are getting many views due to a particular keyword use, you should emulate this.

Analyze and Adapt

Maintaining a successful YouTube business page in the long run is not an easy process. There are instances where you will run out of ideas. After posting for months, there is no guarantee that your posts will still be loved by your followers. To be sure about your marketing efforts, it is vital that you monitor your progress. The good news is that there are metrics to help you do this. A detailed analysis of social media metrics that you should use will be looked at in detail later in the guide.

Snapchat

Snapchat is another vital social platform which is popular among young adults and teens in the United States. One of the main features that make this platform stand out is its ability to easily create multimedia messages, commonly called 'snaps'. Users can create their snaps by combining images, video, and text. The messages can then be shared as stories. Businesses are taking advantage of this feature to create promotional messages.

The social media platform has mainly been adopted by businesses who aim to reach the millennial generation. Accordingly, if you are also looking to attract a huge following composed of mainly of young people, this channel can deliver.

So, which is the right social media platform for your business? Following what has been discussed, there is a lot that you should consider before choosing just any social media channel. The mere fact that a particular platform is ranked among the best in the market doesn't mean it is a good fit for your business. In addition, when looking to emulate what your competitors are doing, always strive to ensure that you learn something from them. Don't just follow them blindly because they are thriving with their marketing campaigns. The digital world is quite unpredictable. As such, it is vital that you develop your marketing strategy by considering your business goals.

Common Social Media Mistakes to Avoid

Sure, picking the best social media platform to suit your business might seem like a straightforward process. However, this leaves us wondering why most people fail in their marketing campaigns. If the process were that easy, then tons of businesses will be boasting about the huge following that they have. Concerning this matter, it is worth taking a look at the common mistakes entrepreneurs make when using social media to promote their brands.

Trying to be Everywhere

When using social media marketing for the first time, you will have the perception that you need to reach to a wide audience. This will influence your decision to use several social media accounts. However, having several social media accounts might not be as effective as you think. In fact, you will only increase pressure on yourself and you might end up giving up if your marketing efforts end up being futile.

So, how do you handle the pressure to attract a large following? Conduct research to find out where your audience has accounts. There is a good chance that your target market will be on more than one social media account. Choose the top three and focus your marketing efforts there. The Pareto Principle works here. Think about it this way, 80% of the followers you will be getting come from 20% of your marketing efforts.[26] Accordingly, there is a lot that you can gain if you choose to prioritize.

Failing to Know Your Audience

Failing to understand your audience on social media will be the beginning of your downfall. You may try everything on social networks, but nothing will seem to favor you. This could happen because you don't know who you are connecting with. Limited knowledge of your audience will have a negative impact on your entire marketing campaign. You will end up choosing the wrong platform to approach them. Additionally, the content you post will not resonate with your followers. Therefore, expect them to unfollow you or ignore your posts altogether.

Failing to Learn from Analytics

Your success in social media marketing will be heavily reliant on how well you study your analytics. Of course, there are certain posts that will be liked more compared to others. It is crucial that you learn something from these posts. Check your posts with the

---

[26] "The 80/20 rule for social media and ideas to help you achieve it ...." 5 Mar. 2018, https://www.shakeitupcreative.com/2018/03/05/the-80-20-rule-for-social-media-and-ideas-to-help-you-achieve-it/. Accessed 2 Aug. 2019.

most likes; what was different about these posts? Did you share funny images or videos? Did you post at a specific time? Learning from your analytics ensures that you post relevant content that appeals to your followers.

Posting Bad Content

Choosing the best platform that works for your business doesn't necessarily mean that you will find it easy to promote content on social media. Content is king. Consequently, posting bad content will only drive traffic away from your end. People want to get value from your posts. So, before posting anything, take a moment to consider whether it is entertaining, informative, and helpful. This is what your audience will be looking for.

Missing Out on Messages and Mentions

Your prospects and customers will easily be discouraged to depend on your brand if you don't respond to their messages promptly. Your audience will be happier to associate with a brand that listens to them. For that reason, you should always ensure that you have a standby team that will respond to queries from your followers.

Forgetting to Test

Throughout your marketing campaign, you will realize that there is a particular marketing formula that works for you. Gaining insight is only possible if you remember to test your advertising technique. For you to experience growth in your company, it is imperative that you continuously test for optimal results. Testing prevents you from making mistakes. You will garner deep insights concerning the best platforms that you should use and those that you should stay away from.

The mistakes which have been discussed are not an exhaustive list of the common mistakes marketers make. Regardless, they should give you a hint of the kind of scrutiny that you ought to embrace in your social media marketing campaign. You should never take anything for granted as it could end up tarnishing your business image. More importantly, never forget that you are on social media to socialize. So, do as the Romans do!

Chapter 4 - Social Media Advertising

Sure, there are a wide array of social media marketing strategies that you might want to adopt. However, social media advertising is what will bring you consistent sales. Social media advertising includes ads posted on social networks for people to access them. The varying social media channels make use of user-generated content to offer the most relevant ads. Such relevance is what ultimately leads to an increase in conversions.

There are several benefits that you will get through social media advertising. Below is a comprehensive look into why social media advertising will offer you the best ROI.

Improved Brand Recognition

Social media ads will enhance your brand recognition. Through this form of advertising, you will be posting more frequently due to the advantage of social media scheduling. Your audience will, therefore, interact with your brand more often and this increases the likelihood of them sharing your content. You should also understand that frequent engagement with your followers gives you a sense of credibility. Ultimately, there is a good chance that they will recommend your products/services to their social circles.

Improved Conversion Rates

As your brand becomes more visible over the internet, this will drive traffic to your business website. Depending on the quality of content that you post, conversion rates will likely increase. Therefore, if your ads are well planned for, you can be sure that you will also boost your returns through increased conversion rates.

Enhanced Brand Loyalty

Besides increasing brand awareness and boosting your conversion rates, your business also stands to benefit from the constant interaction it will have with your followers. In this case, people will have the opportunity to express themselves by sharing their views about your products/services. Listening to your followers can help to enhance brand loyalty since they will be more satisfied. There is no doubt that they will stay loyal to your brand.

Better Search Engine Ranking

Most people have turned to search engines as their ideal source of information when they are looking for products and services to depend on. By posting ads regularly, it means that your brand will be ranked in search engines such as Bing and Google. This will increase your brand's visibility.

Improved Targeting

Another huge benefit of social media advertising is the fact that you can easily narrow down your demographics to specifics such as their location or the devices they are using. Through improved targeting, businesses will end up spending less on advertising. Advertising regularly also gives you the advantage of knowing your customers better. This is because you will be spending time trying to segment the market while engaging in differentiated marketing campaigns.

User-Generated Content

In today's marketing world, the voice of the customer is regarded as a valuable commodity. As businesses continuously interact with their customers, they benefit from the fact that they understand their brand's strengths and weaknesses. Feedback from clients in the market is what makes businesses thrive in their respective markets. This user-generated content should not be taken for granted as it inspires companies to improve their products or service provision, their marketing campaigns, or offer new products. This is a rewarding attribute of social media advertising.

Judging from the benefits outlined, there is a good reason why social media advertising should be included in your social media marketing strategy. It is worth pointing out that posting ads will not bring you immediate results. The process of creating and posting your ads has to be handled strategically. This means that you have to know how much you will be spending on your ads, your targeting frequency, content selection, and channel selection. It is very easy to get confused if you have never advertised on social media. Luckily, you need not to worry as we have done the research for you. The following paragraphs outline the strategic steps you should take when advertising on social media.

Define Your Goals

The first and the most important step that you should take is to define the strategy that you will be using to carry out social media advertising. In other words, what are your advertising goals? What do you aim to accomplish from your advertising? The last thing that you should do is to approach the task blindly since you are likely going to spend a lot of time and money.

Coming up with the right goals and prioritizing them will push you to succeed in your marketing campaign. What are some of these advertising goals that you should set for yourself? Most advertisers will want to achieve the following goals:

Increase Visibility

Visibility of your brand will not only lead to enhanced brand recognition, but it will also bear a positive influence on customer loyalty and purchases. Setting a goal to increase your brand's visibility should be prioritized as it could also boost your impressions and reach.

Increase Traffic

Most new businesses will want to increase traffic to their blogs and their social media homepages. The benefit of increased traffic goes beyond getting better SEO rankings. Your business will also gain from increased sales.

Increase Engagement

You should also set a goal of increasing engagement with your followers. You have to evaluate your engagement levels to determine whether or not your content is working. Some of the metrics that you will be using include likes, shares, comments, retweets, etc. These performance metrics will give you the insights that you need to offer your followers content that resonates with them.

Increase Leads

One of the main reasons why most advertisers use social media ads is to help them increase their leads. Ideally, this is a great way of pulling in new visitors to follow your brand.

Increase Sales

At the end of the day, you aim to increase sales. Undoubtedly, this is what will keep your business running. Accordingly, you will have to work on using different social media advertising options to increase your chances of getting the best out of your marketing campaigns.

Identify Your Audience

Prior to engaging with your followers, you have to identify them. Besides looking at the demographics, you also have to take your time to know their likes and dislikes. This is what will help you to create engaging content. So, where should you start when identifying your target market? Essentially, you should start with the basic aspects of your audience.

- Demographics

With regard to demographics, you will be looking at age groups, average income, location, gender, and so on. Taking this into consideration, you will have to ask yourself whether your target market can afford the product that you are offering. This will push you to focus on a particular group of people with a certain level of income.

In addition, when looking at gender, you should consider whether your product/service suits both men and women. Whilst doing this, you should also contemplate their respective ages and location. These are important demographics which should make it easy for you to know the right people to approach with your ads.

- Psychographics

Psychographics are similar to demographics as they define your audience. However, demographics tend to answer the question of "Who is your audience?" whereas psychographics answer the question "Why would they buy?" Accordingly, psychographics gives you an opportunity to understand your audiences' spending habits, hobbies, and some of their values.

To effectively reach your audience, it is crucial that you garner insights on both their psychographics and demographics. This information will give you a clear picture of the people you are dealing with. Psychographics detail your clients could include the fact that they prefer to live a healthy lifestyle, that they value their time, or that they prefer browsing the internet in the evening or during weekends, etc.

Both psychographics and demographics will also be of great importance when selecting suitable platforms for your marketing campaign. You will want to settle for a platform that offers your followers a seamless shopping experience if they value their time when shopping over the internet.

Pick the Right Social Media Platform

Once you are sure about the goals and audience for your social media marketing strategy, the next thing to do is to choose the right social platforms that will help you meet your goals. When making your decision here, you should keep in mind that there are certain benefits of using one social media channel over the other. Consider whether the platform you choose targets demographics that suit your brand. In addition, you should reflect on whether your market rivals are using the same platform to target customers. That's not all, it is imperative to find out whether your target audience uses the specific channels to engage. More importantly, don't forget to question aspects relating to your ad format. Assess whether the social media network works with the ad format you plan to use such as video, photos, GIFs, etc.

Determining the Right Content

After setting realistic goals, understanding your audience and selecting the right platforms for your advertising campaign, you should work on content. Content is the information that you will be using to engage with your followers and convince them to buy from you. Content will include videos, text, images, infographics, and so on. Good content will make a huge difference in your marketing campaign. Therefore, it is worth learning how to identify the right content to produce. There is no doubt that you will want to create interesting social media ads. The following pointers should help you achieve this.

- GIFs

Who doesn't love to share funny GIFs to their friends? Certainly, we all love to spread the fun on social media through this content. Marketers should keep this in mind when creating GIFs to advertise their brands. Aside from providing valuable information to your audience, they also entertain them.

- Stories

Stories has hit the headlines over the past few years and it has grown to become a popular marketing feature. On Instagram, for example, estimates show that about 500 million people use the story feature every day.[27] This shows that you should consider capitalizing on stories when creating content to post on social networks that offer this feature.

- User-Generated Content

Perhaps you should also contemplate giving your audience a reason to feel that they are part of your brand. There are notable brands out there which take advantage of the opportunity to feature their customers on their social media pages. Posting their images, for instance, says a lot about how they enjoy using your product/service. At the end of the day, they feel as though they are valued and recognized.

- Infographics

When posting ads on social media, your main aim is to make sure that people understand the message you are trying to get across. Consequently, using infographics serves this purpose.

---

[27] "21+ Incredible Instagram Stories Stats to Know in 2019 - 99firms.com." 9 May. 2019, https://99firms.com/blog/instagram-stories-statistics/. Accessed 3 Aug. 2019.

Bringing together pictures and text makes it easy to comprehend what your ads are all about. This is because your audience will have an easier time processing the meaning of your adverts. Instead of just posting text on your Facebook or Twitter page, you can mix text with images. You will appear more persuasive and as a result, gain more followers. To take things up a notch, try bringing your infographics to life by animating them. This is a good idea to ensure that your content is unique and more engaging.

- Shareable Quotes

We all seek inspiration in our everyday lives. As such, posting shareable quotes is a unique way of capturing your audience's attention. By sharing inspiring quotes, you can ensure that they will share them on their social media pages. In addition to increasing user engagement, you will also increase your brand's reach.

- Videos

There is no doubt that videos will drive traffic to your social media page and your business website. Videos tell stories in an engaging way and this is one of the main reasons why people find it easy to share in their social circles. Your limited budget shouldn't hinder you from including video content in your ads. There are plenty of apps which can help you create short and interesting videos.

Select Targeting Options

Social media advertising could easily fail if you do not work on your targeting options. What does this mean? Who you are targeting will have an impact on the response you will get. Targeting a large audience might not be as admirable considering the fact that you cannot be sure that every person you approach will respond positively to your ads. On the contrary, if you focus on a small audience who is more interested in what you are offering, this increases the likelihood of succeeding in your marketing.

The targeting options you will have at your disposal will vary from one social media platform to the other. Let's look at some of these social networks and the targeting options they provide.

Facebook Targeting Options

Facebook, being among the market leaders on social media, has a wide range of targeting options that any marketer will find useful. With these options, it will be easy to reach your intended audience with your promotional messages.

- Demographics

One of the main ways you can use to segment your target market is through demographics. Demographics will help you segment your audience into different categories. Using these options, you can specify your ads to focus on a particular audience. These demographics include:

- Age
- Gender
- Education
- Work
- Location
- Language

Let's use the example of creating an ad for a flower store during Valentine's Day of how you can use demographic targeting to create your ads. Your ad will want to reach local men and women in relationships. In addition, you will want to specify their age bracket. Therefore, you might choose to target individuals aged between 20-25 years old. Your advert will thus be limited to the demographics that you would have specified. This is how such demographics help in narrowing down to a specific audience.

- Interests

Just as the subtitle suggests, targeting your audience based on interests will segment your target market based on what they enjoy. This includes activities such as sports, other hobbies, and fashion tastes. Other specifics categories that you can define here include:

- Business and industry
- Food and drink

- Technology

- Relationships and family

- Entertainment

It goes without saying that these targeting options requires you to understand who your audience is. As such, you will have to create ideal customer profiles before using this feature.

- Life Events

Another targeting option you can use while marketing on Facebook is "Life Events". With this option, businesses can appeal to their audiences during memorable moments that customers celebrate. This means that timing is key when using this targeting option. Some of the events you can focus on here include:

- Birthdays

- Family events - celebrating a newborn or mourning the loss of a family member

- Professional - graduating, a new job, etc.

- Home and Living - purchase of a new home

You have to be specific with your timing when using this targeting option to reach your audience.

- Financial

You can also use Facebook ads to segment your audience based on their income levels. This is a straightforward process since you will only select the option that suits you best depending on your marketing goals.

- Connections

Connections targeting is where a marketer specifies the connection that they share with those they intend to market their brand to. If you choose to use Facebook pages, you can target individuals who have recently liked your page or friends of people who liked your page. Moreover, you have the option of excluding those who liked your page. Concerning apps, you can focus your ads on those who have at least used your app once.

Twitter Targeting Options

Twitter is somewhat different from Facebook in terms of the targeting options that you can use when creating ads. The options that you can use on Twitter include:

- Followers

Here, you can target people who are either following you or those who are following other accounts. Your selection will depend on those who could be interested in your posts.

- Device Targeting

This gives you the opportunity of targeting Twitter users based on the devices they are using.

- Keyword Targeting

Depending on what your prospects are tweeting, you can use this information to specify ads that reach them.

- Geography Targeting

You can also narrow down your target market to people within a particular location.

- Behavior Targeting

Twitter gives you the option of targeting your prospects based on their shopping habits.

The targeting options that you will be using on different social channels should help you segment your market. It makes it easy to narrow down your target market to individuals that are more interested in the products/services you are advertising. Therefore, taking advantage of targeting options gives you the advantage of posting relevant ads. For instance, when you target people based on their lifestyles, people who are more concerned about their health will want to purchase sports-related products. In a way, targeting options increases the likelihood of your ads succeeding.

Chapter 5 - Developing a Social Media Calendar

One of the most important tools you should have in your social media marketing toolkit is a social media calendar. Having a calendar to guide you is the best way in which you can plan your social media campaign. It will help you stay organized as you will know what to post at what time. This means that you will not have to rush to each social media platform wondering what to post. Ultimately, you will find it easy to share quality content with your audience. Your audience will find it worthwhile to engage with your brand. Therefore, there is a good chance that they will recommend your products and services in their social circles.

In an ordinary situation, people use calendars to plan their days, weeks, or months in advance. Doing this ensures that nothing is left unattended to. It should also be noted that the advantage of planning is that it saves a lot of time. Picture a scenario where you failed to plan for your marketing campaign. In this case, you will find yourself scrambling to determine what to post and where to post your content. On the contrary, with a well laid out plan, you would only have to schedule your posts. It makes your social media marketing campaign a straightforward process.

Before discussing the ways in which you can create your social media calendar, it is important that you understand why you should have it.

Why Use a Social Media Calendar?

- Stay Up to Date

It goes without saying that the main reason why you should use a social media calendar is to guarantee that you don't miss important dates. What dates are we talking about here? Throughout your marketing campaign, you will want to take advantage of holidays and other important events. This means that your ads should show that you recognize these dates. Your audience will want to react to your ads based on these calendar events. Thus, it is crucial that you never miss them.

- Consistent Posting Schedule

An important strategy to get more followers to see and like what you post is by posting consistently. You can't post irregularly and still expect people to like or retweet what you are sharing. Individuals on social media look for fresh posts. Accordingly, they will be discouraged to follow your brand if your last posts are dated back to a couple of weeks ago.

That's not all, consistent posting also gives your audience the impression that they can interact with you more often. If your posts are frequent, they will be convinced that they can interact with your brand anytime they want. This is a good first impression which will help you win over a huge following.

- Effective Allocation of Resources

A social media calendar also gives you the opportunity of apportioning your resources in a desirable manner. You should never forget that you might not work alone in your social media marketing campaign. Depending on the size of your company, you will want to hire copywriters, video editors, designers, etc. Planning helps you in knowing how best your company's resources will be utilized. In the end, a good plan will save you from wasting your resources.

- Determining Your Content Mix

A social media content calendar will also make it easy for you to know the right content that suits your audience. Remember, people are not on social media channels to watch you talk about your brand and nothing else. It is crucial that you find a balance between promoting your brand and interacting with your audience. A calendar will assist you in scheduling different kinds of posts including user-generated content, videos, curated articles, etc.

- Avoid Posting Errors Across Platforms

Let's face it, we are human beings capable of making mistakes. Marketers might be confused when creating and posting ads on different social media pages. One could easily get confused and ask their Facebook audience to "retweet" their shared ads. On the other hand, it is a common mistake to ask your audience to follow you on a particular social media network when you don't have an account there.

A social media calendar could save you from these cross-platform mistakes. This is because you will be planning in advance. Accordingly, it will be easy to determine whether the posts created suit their intended platforms.

Now that you understand why a content calendar is important in your social media campaign, let's delve into the most effective ways of creating the calendar.

Conduct a Social Media Audit

First things first, conduct a social media audit to determine how you use different social media channels. Here, you should be aware of the social media platforms you prefer to use. Moreover, your audit should settle on the channels that perform well. Your posting frequency to the respective social accounts should also be determined here.

Setting and Identifying Your Cadence

Another important step that you will want to take is to work on your content cadence. Your cadence on social media is the voice that you will be using to market your brand. It aids your audience to visualize the message that you are trying to pass across. Better yet, cadence will also guarantee that your content is both informative and educative. You should understand that the right cadence will draw your audience to the ads you will post.

There are various questions that you ought to address when setting your cadence. Some of these questions include:

- Who is your target audience?
- How does your target audience prefer to be communicated with?
- What type of content will be more suitable for your audience?
- What will happen after your visitor responds to a CTA?
- What is the next step if a visitor fails to respond?

The questions listed above should help a marketer in setting triggers which should be used throughout their marketing campaign. These triggers define how you will conduct your campaign activities. For example, if a prospect responds to a call to action, the marketer should provide relevant links to direct them. Similarly, if they fail to respond, the right marketing tactics should be used to make sure that prospects are not discouraged from sharing your ads.

An important consideration that should be kept in mind is that cadence focuses more on how you communicate with your followers. Indeed, your style of communication will play a crucial part in engaging with your audience. Bearing this in mind, your cadence should address issues such as:

- Frequency - Here, you will want to find out the number of posts that your followers can comfortably engage with daily or monthly. You shouldn't forget the fact that social media channels have different recommended limits. So, they will vary.

- Timing - Timing is key to ensure that your content reaches your intended audience at the right time. For that reason, your cadence should address the best times of the day that you should post.

- Length - It is vital to know the way in which your followers consume content. Some people prefer short videos whereas others prefer long videos. Ensure that you know how your target market prefers the length of your posts to be.

- Personality - Personality also matters a great deal as people have varying expectations. Your aim should be to provide your audience with what they need without compromise.

Prepare a Social Promotion Request Form

As you strive to gain more followers on social media, you may have to create a social media promotion request form. This request form gives your customers the opportunity to request content from you. Your promotion request form will vary depending on how you want it to appear on your social media posts. For instance, you can choose to use pop-ups. With this option, the request form will appear at a specified time when a user views your ad. Often, request forms appear either at the beginning, in the middle, or at the end of your post.

Posting Frequency on Social Networks

A crucial decision that you will have to make is determining your posting frequency. There are several factors that you should remember to reflect on including your audience, your company size, social channels being used, and the specifications of your campaign.

When reflecting on the type of business you are running, you should compare your marketing efforts alongside your rivals. If you are in an industry where companies post more often due to the competitive nature of the business, then you will also be forced to post frequently. Different businesses have varying goals. Therefore, the frequency of your posts will be influenced by the goals that you wish to accomplish. When looking to boost brand awareness, you should consider posting several times a day. Additionally, you should embrace the importance of posting on different social channels to increase your brand's visibility.

More importantly, you should never forget to contemplate on what your audience wants to see from you. What kind of posts do they love to see? What are some of the products and services that they are looking for? Bearing this in mind helps to make sure that you don't overload your target audience with content that they deem inappropriate.

Similarly, you should think about the number of followers that you are dealing with. For a business with a huge following, they will have to find a way of ensuring that they enhance their organic reach while still maintaining their brand's visibility online. Determining the right number of social media posts to reach a larger portion of your audience is key.

As mentioned earlier, your posting frequency will be heavily dependent on the type of campaigns that you run. Most people get caught up in the notion of frequency and they end up assuming that posting more often will increase their chances of succeeding. This is far from the truth because it does not take into consideration the quality of your campaigns. Just posting ads on social media because you should post doesn't guarantee you the results you are looking for. In fact, there is a possibility that your audience will feel irritated as you would be flooding their social media pages.

A mixture of different types of posts is the best way of keeping your followers engaged. Instead of just posting image ads, you should combine this with videos and infographics. In the end, your followers will not only be entertained, but they will also find your content helpful. Thus, they will want to be associated with your brand. This leads to an increase in followers.

With regard to social media networks, posting frequency will differ. The following is a succinct look into different social channels and their respective posting frequencies.

Facebook

Facebook has recently updated its algorithm to ensure that businesses interact with their audiences without nagging them. Therefore, the algorithm strives to reduce noise on social media pages by promoting organic content. Studies show that the optimal posting frequency for Facebook is once a day.[28] A maximum of two posts is also considered ideal. The point here is that you should understand that "less is more."

You might have the assumption that posting up to five times a day is the best way of reaching your audience. The reality is that

---

[28] "How Often To Post On Social Media According To 14 ... - CoSchedule." 18 Oct. 2017, https://coschedule.com/blog/how-often-to-post-on-social-media/. Accessed 6 Aug. 2019.

the Facebook algorithm will limit how these posts are seen by your audience. So, it is best that you stick with one or two posts a day. You should not post less than 3 times a week.

Several studies find that posting in the afternoon is the best time to post on Facebook. You should post between 1 p.m. and 4 p.m.

Regardless of the recommended times proposed, you should do your homework and evaluate the times when your audience are most active on this platform. You should settle for the most appropriate time which works for your audience. It's not about posting when you are free or when you find convenient. Your target market is more important. So, aim to find out when they are usually online.

Twitter

Unlike Facebook, you will have to post several times a day on your Twitter business page. The recommended number of times is 15 times a day.[29] Your tweets should be evenly spread throughout the day. However, most people would disagree with this posting schedule since top accounts post more than 50 times a day. Again, the aspect of the size of your business comes into play here. As a market entrant, you may have to consider

---

[29] "How Often To Post On Social Media According To 14 … - CoSchedule."

increasing your posting rate gradually. One of the main reasons why there are many tweets posted in this platform is because of the short life span of posts. Accordingly, posting more often could increase your social media reach.

Instagram

The posting schedule of Instagram is somewhat similar to that of Facebook. A marketer should make sure that their posts do not exceed three a day. This means that limiting your posts to two a day is ideal. Posting in the morning around 8 a.m. to 9 a.m. and in the afternoon at 2 a.m. is advisable for Instagram.[30] But then again, you should remember to evaluate your audience to figure out the best posting schedule.

Pinterest

For Pinterest, 11 pins a day are recommended. A minimum of 3 and a maximum of 30 pins are required.[31] For a new business,

---

[30] "How Often To Post On Social Media According To 14 ... - CoSchedule."

[31] "How Often To Post On Social Media According To 14 ... - CoSchedule." 18 Oct. 2017, https://coschedule.com/blog/how-often-to-post-on-social-media/. Accessed 6 Aug. 2019.

one should start with a few pins and track the progress of the campaigns. If they are not yielding the best results, you should consider increasing the number of pins you use. Of course, you shouldn't overlook the fact that the relevance of your posts will have an impact on the success of your campaign.

LinkedIn

Interestingly, LinkedIn is not as demanding compared to Facebook, Twitter, Instagram, and the likes. One post a day is enough to reach your audience. You should schedule this post between 10 a.m. and 11 a.m. for best results.

YouTube

Frankly, posting on YouTube is time-consuming. There is a lot that you will have to work on to ensure that your posts are the best quality. Sure, you can upload your YouTube videos any day during the week. However, the best time to do this is from Thursday to Friday. Consider posting in the afternoon between 12 noon and 3 p.m.

Snapchat

Snapchat is an ideal platform to use if you are looking to target Millenials. About five posts a day is good for this social channel. Marketers can also skip a day when they feel they lack quality content to share with their audience.

Evidently, varying posting schedules should be used on different social media channels. Appropriate timing should not be neglected as it determines whether your posts will reach the intended audience. It should be made clear that there is no one size fits all with regard to posting on social media pages. You cannot assume that you will be posting in the morning on all your business social media profiles. It is prudent to stick to proven statistics on how people often use their social media accounts. This lowers the likelihood of failing in your campaign. More importantly, evaluation should be done often to determine whether your efforts are paying off. Through such evaluation, a marketer can make adjustments that will see their marketing campaign flourish.

Social Media Daily Checklist

The advantage of having a social media calendar is that you will always stay on top of your marketing campaign. At no time will you find yourself confused about what you should post.

Generally, you will find it easier to get things done with minimal effort. Apart from using a calendar, you should also have a daily checklist by your side.

Perhaps you are wondering why it is imperative for you to own a daily checklist. There is a lot that you will be doing to market your brand on social media. This means that there are some basic tasks which might slip your mind and you could easily forget to handle them. That's not all, a checklist helps you to stay organized. You will prioritize your daily tasks based on urgency and importance. As such, you will work on what's important first as you schedule other tasks for a later time.

You should also think about the benefits of maintaining your consistency. A checklist will ensure that everything that needs to be done is accomplished within the day. Most people struggle with consistency simply because there are mundane activities which sometimes take up most of their time. Before you notice, the day has ended and there are important tasks which have not been completed. So, a checklist prevents this from happening since you are always on track on what needs to be done to uphold your performance coherence.

Marketers should also realize that checklists help in the successful delegation of tasks. Since you will be working as a team, you should know how to assign tasks to the right people. This is what a checklist will help you do. At the end of the day, you will know whether tasks have been completed based on the delegation criteria you deemed appropriate.

Clearly, a checklist is a handy tool to assist you in your social media advertising campaign. So, what should your daily checklist feature? The following list gives you an idea of how your everyday routine should look like in terms of social media marketing.

- Reply to messages and questions
- Check mentions on social pages
- Track keywords
- Check all social media profiles
- Identify industry trends
- Check rival posts
- Identify trending hashtags
- Track and reply to influencers' posts
- Follow back

Ordinarily, these tasks seem easy, right? Well, the reality is that you can forget to attend to them when you have a lot on your plate. Usually, this occurs for business owners who run their social media campaigns on their own. Moreover, considering the fact that social media advertising is demanding, you could get overwhelmed with what needs to be done. Ultimately, there is a chance that you could forget one or two things on your list. In that case, you shouldn't ignore the importance of working with a daily checklist.

Besides creating a daily checklist, you should also consider working with a weekly and monthly checklist. Your weekly checklist will feature more demanding activities including:

- Check your stats

- Engage with partners/influencers

- Check weekly goals

- Update social media ads

- Identify best performing posts

Are you still skeptical about the idea of using a social media calendar? Following what has been discussed in this section, using a calendar helps you to stay on top of your game. Timing is very important in social media marketing. It can make or break your brand on social media. With the help of a practical calendar, you will always post at the right time and in the recommended frequency. Without a doubt, the last thing you need is for your audience to have the perception that you are unresponsive or inactive on social media.

Better yet, you've also garnered insights on why you should have a daily checklist. There are times when it is difficult to remember everything relating to your marketing campaign. You should remember that you will also focus on your everyday hustle and bustle to earn a living. For that reason, there is a lot that needs to be done which calls for an organized way of doing so using a checklist.

Chapter 6 - How to Structure Your Social Media Team

With over 2 billion people active on social media, it shows that your business stands to benefit by having an active social media presence.[32] Social media channels including Facebook, Instagram, Twitter, LinkedIn, YouTube, and Snapchat provide you with a wide market to target in your marketing campaign. Marketing your brand on these social media pages isn't just about posting content and responding to your followers. Besides posting information to these accounts, you also need to manage your marketing campaign. This entails knowing what to post and the right platforms to use. More importantly, it also centers around working with the right social media team.

The structure of your social media team will have an impact on your business' success or failure. This section takes a look at some of the most important considerations when structuring your team.

---

[32] "Social Media Platforms and Demographics - LSE." https://info.lse.ac.uk/staff/divisions/communications-division/digital-communications-team/assets/documents/guides/A-Guide-To-Social-Media-Platforms-and-Demographics.pdf. Accessed 6 Aug. 2019.

Evaluate Your Current Situation

A crucial step that you ought to take before doing anything else is to ponder on your current situation. This is because there are a number of factors which will have an impact on the decisions you will be making. Your budget, for example, will influence the number of people you will choose to hire. Additionally, this will affect the social media marketing tools that you will utilize.

You should also spend some time evaluating the team that you currently have. A small company will want to cut on its overcall costs by using their current team if they are qualified to handle certain tasks. What's more, going over the resources that you can use in your marketing campaign can help a lot in knowing what you need to successfully conduct a marketing campaign.

Creating a Social Media Governance Board

You will want to have a team of professionals capable of delivering their best concerning the social media marketing project at hand. In addition to this, you should think about creating a governance board. This is a board which comprises of stakeholders and executives who oversee the whole marketing campaign. Their job is to make sure that everything runs smoothly and according to the company's goals. In your absence, they should provide directives to ensure that challenging situations are properly dealt with.

The following are pointers to help you in creating a social media governance board.

Determining the Governance Members

The first step towards creating a social media governance board is to determine who you want to serve here. Regardless of the fact that you might have people who are qualified in various ways, it doesn't guarantee that they are the right fit. Your selection should be based on key people in your social media marketing strategy. The main thing that you will be looking for here is people with the ability to foster the right direction in your marketing campaign. Some individuals you can include here are content managers, executives, directors, etc.

Create a Board Charter

After coming up with a list of people who will be serving in the governance board, your next move should be to schedule a meeting with them. During this meeting, you should discuss the goals and missions of the governance board. The outcome of your meeting would be the creation of fundamental principles that govern this board. Roles and responsibilities should also be a topic of discussion in this meeting. Generally, the significance of this meeting is to make sure that every board member knows what they should do to enhance productivity in your company.

Clarify Social Media Goals

Once the board members are made aware of their respective duties and responsibilities, the next thing is to clarify strategic social media goals. Here, the focus will be on determining the current social performance of the company and the marketing direction that it will be taking.

Break up the Project into Stages

There are varying social media marketing techniques that companies can use to reach their goals. Nonetheless, it is a prudent idea to breakdown the process into stages. The significance of this strategy is that it makes the marketing campaign easy to handle. So, instead of posting content on various social networks, it is a brilliant idea to divide the whole marketing campaign into stages.

Communicating Goals and Training Staff

The governance board is responsible for communicating the social media goals to training staff on how the set goals can be achieved. As the business owner, you should be there to meet with the board members and discuss more on the social media goals. You want to be on the same page with these stakeholders which means that your presence is of great importance.

Once you are sure that your governance board is ready, the next thing should be to communicate to the rest of your social media team. Other employees should also be trained on how they will be operating. This includes knowing where they should seek clarification whenever they feel stuck.

Your governance board should not forget the importance of meeting regularly to evaluate the company's progress with regard to set goals. Depending on the size of your team, these meetings can be scheduled weekly or monthly.

Staffing Considerations

There is a lot to consider when creating your social media team. Most new social media marketers will jump to the conclusion that one should only take into consideration the qualifications of your new team members. While this is an important factor to think about, it is not the only thing that you will be examining when putting together your social media team. Other factors that will influence your staffing are discussed below.

Budget for New Employees

Your new staff budget will definitely affect the number of people that you will be recruiting. If you are running on a tight budget, you will have to settle for a few employees capable of meeting your social media goals. As previously mentioned, some companies will want to cut down on their expenditure by opting to work with current employees to fill up the social media positions.

You should never focus on looking for cheaper hires because of the limited budget you have. Undeniably, this will only push you to settle for less. Moreover, it increases the likelihood of going for the wrong people. Therefore, strive to hire fewer people who are qualified instead of trying to save money by looking for people who are underqualified.

Strategic Goals

The strategic goals of your social media campaign will have a huge impact on the people you will be choosing to work on your social media campaign team. In most cases, this will affect your team's size. The bigger the goals you are looking to accomplish, the bigger your team should be. Moreover, if your company places high regard for the importance of social media marketing, then there is a good chance that you will want a big team.

Skills Required

When choosing members for your social media team, you should consider the skills that you are looking for in your marketing team. Some of the positions that you should fill when making your team selection include:

- Social Media Manager

An individual taking on this role will be responsible for creating a social media marketing strategy. For a small company, a social media manager will take on most of the responsibilities regarding social media including coordinating social media accounts, social listening, publishing content, and responding to comments.

- Content Creators

Content creators will also form an integral part of your social media team. These are the people who will work to make sure that content posted resonates with your target audience. In addition, their responsibility will be to deliver quality content that could easily encourage the audience to like, share, or retweet. Considering the fact that content is king in your social media campaign, you shouldn't ignore the importance of hiring content creators.

- Community Manager

Another crucial member of your team will be the community manager. The role of this person is to engage with your target audience. This means that they should be there to resolve any negative publicity related to your brand. Their efforts will be required to make certain that social media engagement is given a boost.

- Analyst

Evaluating your social media performance will contribute a lot to the success of your business. Often, this is made possible by using performance metrics such as traffic, engagement rates, conversions, shares etc. If you lack the required skills to track and understand how performance can be improved, then you should not forget to hire someone to do the job.

Social Media Platforms to be Used

Once you have determined the people that you will be working with, you should also take a moment to think about the platforms that you will be using. Certainly, there are tons of social media networks out there. It is crucial that you settle for the best fit for your business.

In line with choosing the most appropriate platform for your business demands, marketers might end up concluding that they should have more members to oversee different social media accounts. Sure, this might appear as a desirable move. However, there are problems that you could face including collaboration issues and consistency in your brand's voice. Accordingly, hiring more people to help you manage the different social media profiles you have is not always a wise strategy.

Fortunately, there are several social media management applications which can be used to reduce the management workload by bringing together social media profiles on one platform. More on these metrics will be discussed later on in this manual.

Content Strategy

The content strategy that you will adopt will also have an impact on your staffing decisions. If you are going to create high-quality content, it means that you will have to consider hiring experts for the job. Creation of videos, for example, is quite demanding. If you don't have the required skills to create interesting videos, then it is likely that people will not like your content. Therefore, as part of creating a good social media team, you have to hire skilled individuals to create the quality content that you are looking for.

Choosing the structure of your social media team will depend a lot on what you think works for your company. Regardless, there are a number of responsibilities that you should remember to cover. First, your social media team should align with the company's overall goals. It is also vital that you clarify the social media marketing objectives with your team. That's not all - social channel optimization and the content strategy to be utilized should be clearly defined for the team to work effectively. Without a plan, it will be difficult for you to coordinate campaign activities meant to promote your brand on social media. More importantly, social analytics will come in handy as they ensure that you know whether you are performing well or not.

Chapter 7 - Integrating Social Media into Your Omnichannel Marketing Strategy

The advent of the internet has brought profound changes in the world today. It can be argued that the internet has given a huge boost to technological innovations. Today, there are numerous devices that people can use to purchase products over the internet. Their shopping experience is even made more convenient since they can order products from their social media pages and collect these goods from physical stores. What this means is that the shopping experience for customers has been transformed as they not only find it convenient to shop using social media apps, but they also fancy the idea that products are closer to them than ever before. Omnichannel marketing strategy centers around the idea of providing clients with a seamless and integrated shopping experience in all the marketing channels used by a particular company.

The competitive nature of businesses today should influence companies to strive and meet customer demands without bias. In this case, it doesn't matter where a customer is shopping, what matters is that they get the products that they purchased online. This means that businesses should work to seamlessly integrate both online and physical stores. For an optimal omnichannel experience, it is imperative that social platforms should also be integrated to work harmoniously. Ultimately, this leads to a huge boost in consumer engagement.

Today, we have seen businesses benefit from the fact that they are integrating social media marketing into other marketing channels that they are using. The best part is that these businesses win over the hearts and minds of their customers. In the real sense, if a customer finds it convenient to shop from their phone and get the products delivered to a physical store that they can easily access, there is a good chance that they will shop more. On the contrary, single-channel customers will not be as motivated to shop as those who have experienced the benefits of omnichannel marketing.

Digitally speaking, omnichannel customers are more proficient in the way in which they use their devices to shop. Interestingly, they are also more willing to spend compared to customers who have not been through an omnichannel experience. Often, omnichannel clients can engage anywhere and still purchase products. For that reason, it is vital that businesses should obtain and integrate insights that they get from multi-channel analytics and from their social media marketing. This is the best way to deliver exceptional customer experience that will also benefit them in the long run.

An important fact that should be made clear about the integration of omnichannel marketing with social media is that price is not a factor that influences people's shopping habits. If retailers ignore their customers and fail to place importance on their shopping experience, there is a good chance they will suffer. People will want to depend on a brand that provided them with a great shopping experience regardless of the price tags on their products/services. So, blending social media marketing with an omnichannel marketing strategy has little to do with price.

What is Omnichannel Marketing?

Maybe you are still racking your brain trying to figure out what omnichannel marketing means. This refers to a marketing approach which brings together varying communication channels used by businesses to reach their customers.[33] Businesses use customer interests and perspectives on brands or specific products and services to optimize their marketing messages. Ultimately, this helps them to maintain consistency in all their marketing channels. The result of this is that it increases the effectiveness of marketing campaigns.

There are numerous ways in which we have enjoyed an omnichannel experience. In the banking industry, for example, there are certain banks which have taken steps to ensure that

---

[33] "12 Examples of Brands With Brilliant Omni-Channel ... - HubSpot Blog." 21 Mar. 2019, https://blog.hubspot.com/service/omni-channel-experience. Accessed 6 Aug. 2019.

their customers can enjoy all their services from the convenience of their mobile application. In this case, you can easily schedule appointments as well as deposit a check without having to visit the bank in person. The same can be done for payment of bills and other monthly expenses.

In addition, there are loyalty programs offered by brands as a way of enticing their prospects and loyal customers. Usually, these programs are simply incentives which are meant to motivate people to purchase more of a particular product or depend on a certain service. Such exciting shopping experience gives a customer a reason to maintain their loyalty with a particular brand.

Tips to Successfully Integrate Social Media into Your Omnichannel Marketing Strategy

To guarantee that you maximize the benefits that come with blending social media into your omnichannel marketing strategy, the following points should be considered.

Engage in Social Listening

An effective way of knowing your customers on social media is by engaging in social listening. This gives you the opportunity to find out exactly where they engage with their friends on social media pages. That's not all, you will also gain insight on conversations about your industry and your brand. Analyzing the insights that you get on your customers helps you meet customer expectations as you will deliver just what they are looking for. Keeping this in mind, adding in what you learn from social listening will undeniably enhance both your products and service provision in all the marketing channels you use.

Mixing Social Media and Email Marketing

Bringing together social media and email marketing can also be a great strategy to boost engagement in your marketing campaign. How do you do this? You should consider promoting your social media pages using email. Here, you should encourage your customers to get more information about your brand by visiting your social media profiles. Remember, you should make this easy for them by adding social media buttons on the emails you send.

The same marketing strategy can also be adopted on your social media pages. Your posts should encourage people by offering them freebies once they opt to sign up for your newsletters.

Centralize the Data Collected

Social media pages provide you with a wide array of information about your customers. This means that you can make good use of this information to personalize your promotional messages. Besides knowing more about your clients' tastes and preferences, you are also informed about their hobbies, shopping habits, health perceptions, and lifestyle choices, etc.

With all the information that you get from your clients, it is crucial that you create a complete profile featuring your specific target audience. This is where the use of customer relationship management (CRM) software comes in handy. With the help of this tool, you can gather and centralize your customer information. The advantage gained here is that your social media team can work harmoniously across different social media platforms.

Never Ignore Your Audience

The last thing that you should do to your prospects is ignore them. This is something that you might be tempted to do more so when they are responding negatively to your social media posts. Ignoring these negative messages will not solve anything. It is vital that you respond to everything on your social media account. This is what engagement is all about.

Your team should be well-trained to use tools that help monitor all conversations relating to your brand. This is the best way to not miss out on anything which could tarnish your brand's image.

Support In-App Purchases

An exceptional strategy to providing your clients with an omnichannel experience is by merging your business website to your social networks. This gives your prospects and customers the ability to purchase products through their social networks. Your clients do not need to necessarily visit your business website to make purchases. Integrated links on your social media posts will automate the process for them.

Encourage Recommendations

People will want to buy your products if there are recommendations from friends in their social circle. For that reason, you should encourage testimonials from other customers who have used your product/service. Don't make it difficult for customers to tell other people about their shopping experience with your brand. Include convenient share buttons after completing transactions. This way, they will find sharing easy as they only need to make a few clicks to recommend your brand in their social circles. The same case applies if you prefer to give your customers an opportunity to leave their feedback. Aim to make the process easy for them.

Cross-Channel Social Media Marketing with Marketing Automation

Technology has indeed brought about numerous changes in the way people communicate. People always strive to be connected using social media. It is therefore not surprising to find people interacting on their social media profiles and checking their emails throughout the day. We have smartphones to help us remain connected and help us stay up to date with what is happening around us. In fact, the use of smartphones has become a norm even in the workplace and most social settings.

Businesses have to face the challenge of penetrating through all the noise and delivering their messages to their intended prospects and customers. Now, this is where cross-channel social media marketing comes in. This refers to a marketing approach where brands find an effective way of seamlessly communicating with their prospects and customers across multiple channels.

Through this marketing approach, there are several benefits that they could gain. Some of these are succinctly discussed in the following paragraphs.

Before getting into detail concerning the benefits of cross-channel social media marketing, it is important to understand that this approach is different from multi-channel marketing.

Most people will confuse the two terms and therefore, it is essential that you draw a line between the two.

A multi-channel marketing approach concerns the idea of having an online presence on several channels. In this case, brands can have an online presence using a mobile application and a business website. On the contrary, a cross-channel strategy refers to an approach where brands provide their customers with a seamless experience on all the different channels that they are using to market their brand.

A good example of how this works is when customers use the internet to research brands and products that they can rely on. Often, brands will find a way of reaching these customers through email applications on their smartphones. Therefore, there is a continuous experience that a shopper will experience as brands move from one channel to another without actually interrupting the customer. Some of the pros of this form of marketing strategy include:

Increasing Engagement

Cross-channel social media marketing with marketing automation will often lead to an increase in the engagement levels between brands and their customers. The idea of using multiple marketing channels to reach customers means that you will be interacting with them throughout the day. For instance, when customers are accessing their emails and updating their social accounts. Brands remain connected with their prospects in all the stages of their purchasing cycle. Therefore, it would be easy to remind a consumer that they did not complete a particular purchase they were interested in.

Enhanced Loyalty

The consistency that a cross-channel marketing approach offers gives customers an easier way of reaching out to brands. This is because they are always kept updated with new products/services that brands are planning to introduce to the market. Discounts and other product information which could benefit them are some of the things that they are always informed about. Consequently, such interaction could drive customers to become loyal to a particular brand.

Align with Consumer Behavior

Another major benefit of the cross-channel marketing approach is that it aligns with consumer behaviors in many ways. Today, brands have to deal with customers using different forms of technology to communicate. In addition to this, brands also need to up their game and make sure that they seamlessly merge online and offline marketing channels. The diverse nature of the customer in the way they consume information means that it is a great idea for companies to utilize a cross-channel marketing strategy.

In spite of the benefits that companies could accrue through the use of cross-channel marketing, there are several barriers that they will have to deal with.

Disintegrating Silos

A huge barrier that brands have to overcome is the fact that they have to break down existing working structures in the company. Normally, companies will have different teams to handle varying aspects of social media. Some will deal with social platforms, while others run the business' website, and a few of them will work on emails. The problem here is that it becomes difficult to achieve consistency in the brand's voice. Accordingly, companies will have to work on disintegrating these structures and find coherence in how they operate.

Limitations in Technology

Technology is ever-changing. This could have an impact on brands as they may struggle to adapt to the new changes that they have to put up with. For instance, adjusting to a new social channel might not be easy as brands will have to learn more about the social platform and how their customers use it.

Luckily, there are practical ways of making sure that cross-channel social media marketing is automated for optimal results.

Plan Ahead Using a Marketing Calendar

The success of your social media marketing campaign is heavily dependent on how well you plan it. There are numerous things that should be considered in your social media marketing efforts. As such, it is important that you rely on a marketing calendar. This guarantees that you maintain a consistent voice on all the social media platforms that you are using. Ideally, this is an effective way to get customers to fall in love with your brand and help them find it convenient to engage with you.

Ensure All Content is Shareable

One of the main benefits of promoting your brand on social media is that it increases user engagement. This can be given a boost by incorporating the use of social media buttons in all the content that you share. You have the option of using either paid or free versions of these buttons depending on your marketing goals and your marketing budget. However, you should understand that there will be certain limitations when you opt for free versions. This is because you will not be in a position to customize your messaging or effectively track how your content is being shared on different social media platforms.

Focus on the Customer

Regardless of the fact that you will be using different platforms to interact with your target market, it is crucial that you focus on the customer. Informing your social media team about this also ensures that you maintain a consistent voice in the varying social media pages you will be using. The good news is that all your brand's marketing efforts will be tailored to making sure that customers' needs are met. Customers don't want to get distracted by similar brands when you're engaging with them. Accordingly, it is vital that your omnichannel marketing approach upholds consistency by providing your audience a seamless shopping experience.

Make Good Use of Data Collected

Data collected from various social media pages will provide you with the insight that you require to serve your customers better. This makes it imperative for you to collect and assess data to understand your audience's shopping habits, tastes and preferences, lifestyle choices, and what they like or dislike. Remember, gathering all this information in a single database is the best way to personalize your marketing messages and capture your audience's attention. So, do remember to centralize the data storage process.

Brands should take advantage of the fact that the can incorporate social media marketing in their omnichannel marketing strategy. With the diverse nature of the clientele that companies have to deal with, they should aspire to meet their needs. Undeniably, this will not be an easy feat. This doesn't mean that it is impossible. There are numerous data analysis tools that can be used to study your customers' behaviors on social media. You can then use this information to deliver personalized messages that will keep them engaged with your brand. You should realize that this is the direction that most businesses are heading. Therefore, for you to remain competitive in your industry, you should consider bringing in social media to your omnichannel marketing strategy.

Chapter 8 - Your Social Media Technology Stack

Social networking applications have become the norm in today's world. More and more people are looking for ways of communicating using these applications. Interestingly, the same communication trend is constantly being adopted by businesses as they need to provide their customers a better way of engaging with them. Notable brands have been on the frontline in coming up with applications to facilitate engagement with their client base.

Developing a Social Media App

Developing social media apps has a three-tier structure that includes the mobile customer/client, backend, and database. Let's start by taking a look at the respective sections.

Customer/Client

There are three basic features that your social media application should feature when describing your target audience.

- Profiles

Any new customer that wants to use your mobile application will start by creating their profile. This makes it important for developers to consider incorporating a database that defines who the customer is. Without a user profile, it would be difficult for clients to connect with each other. Creating a user profile is not as difficult as you might think. The easiest way of doing this is by linking the user profiles to their respective social media pages. For instance, a user's Facebook or Twitter profile can be used to set up the profile.

An important thing that you should remember is that people enjoy the idea of looking good on social media. It is for this reason that your developers should work to provide alternative ways of customizing their profiles. For instance, you should consider providing your audience with photo effects, background colors, exciting theme settings and links to their websites that they can add.

- Connections

Social media application users will want to utilize the advantage of interacting with other people on the social platform that you provided them. Accordingly, your developers have to provide a way for users to engage with and follow others. There are a number of ways in which you can help users connect with each other.

- Groups

People love the idea of joining groups because they have the opportunities to meet people who share similar values. Therefore, your social media application should provide this feature. Creation of groups on your social media app doesn't have to be based on user profiles alone. The groups can also bring together other businesses that yearn to be part of your growing social media platform. For instance, the app can have a Facebook or Twitter page that brings together individuals on these pages.

- Events

Engaging with people can also be based on real life events outside the digital platform. The application can, therefore, be used as a platform where people plan functions. Your app will help its users to move from digital communication to real-life interaction.

- Engaging Content

People can also come together by interacting with the content that you share. Depending on how people choose to interact, there are those who will prefer to comment on what you are sharing, and others who want to use your application to search for new content. Consequently, providing them with a feed will be a great way of keeping them engaged.

- Recommendations

In addition, it would be a great idea for you to give recommendations to your app users. This gives them an opportunity to make new connections depending on what they are searching for or based on their mutual friends. This is something that you must have come across if you have ever used Facebook to connect.

- Feeds

Apart from profiles and connections, your business social media application should consider having feeds. Without feeds, your application will not be engaging. It is through these feeds that users can like and share content posted on other social networks. Usually, feeds entail user-generated content including photos, videos, audio, and presentations. Social media users will want to share their content for various reasons. Some of them include:

- Self-Expression

When using social media, people want to express their personalities using photos, videos, text, and other forms of infographics. Your social media application should make it easy for people to create and share content. User-generated content will give your application the advantage of attracting more followers since more and more people will be curious to join.

- Self-esteem

Social media users often aspire to look good in front of their peers. Therefore, the best way of allowing users to show off is by rewarding them for their engagement activities. Usually, social applications will provide certain badges to show particular rankings of users. This makes them feel good about themselves and maintain their social media engagement levels.

- Status Updates

Common user-generated content that will bring people together is status updates. This is where other users update each other about what they are doing or where they are located. The most important consideration that you should keep in mind is providing app users with a straightforward way of sharing updates or tagging locations.

Backend

Developers of your social media application should aim to create a social application that is not only secure but also scalable. Using a solid backend warrants that your application is efficient. The technical aspects of your application should be effectively handled by skilled personnel.

Database

It is also vital that you use a scalable database. Just like the backend, this is an area that should be well taken care of by hiring technical experts.

Social Media and Marketing Automation

The idea of automating certain activities in your social media campaign might sound controversial. This is because social media is all about being social with your prospects and customers. However, the reality is that there are specific tasks that you can automate. Throughout your marketing campaign, there is no doubt that you will want to make your work easier. This means using automation tools that will help you enjoy promoting your brand on social media.

Marketing automation doesn't mean that you should automate everything. The idea is to find a way of effectively engaging with your target audience without making them feel as though they are interacting with robots. Therefore, such automation should be done in the right way. In line with this, it is crucial to take a look into some of the dos and don'ts when automating certain aspects of your marketing campaign.

Don't Send Automated Direct Messages

Your social media business page will be an excellent platform for your audience to engage with your brand. Customers will therefore expect to interact by asking questions relating to your brand. The last thing that you should do is to automate the conversations you have with them. Frankly, this leaves your clients feeling ignored. When this happens, rest assured that your rivals will take advantage of the situation and offer your prospects with what they are looking for.

Do Have Authentic Conversations

In conjunction with what has been said above, it should be your priority to humanize your social media platform as much as possible. This means that you should get rid of the idea that you should post on social media and then forget about it. When customers respond to your posts or mention your brand name on social media, you should be courteous enough to respond thoughtfully.

Running a large business is not an excuse to ignore some of your customers. You should realize that information on social media spreads like wildfire. So, the last thing you need is to risk ignoring a particular complaint from one of your clients in the hopes that they might give up. A good move would be to hire the best team to handle basic tasks within your social media campaign.

Don't Buy Followers

With the hype surrounding having many followers on your social media page, you might be tempted to buy followers. This is not a good idea as buying followers only gets you the numbers. It should be noted that having many followers doesn't help you in any way as it will not promote engagement. It is better to have fewer quality followers who will find your social media ads relevant. So, don't waste your time and money buying followers. Instead, strive for quality engagement with the prospects and customers that you have.

Do Maintain Consistency in Your Posting Routine

The best way of attracting a large following for your brand is by posting at the right time and on the right platform. Ideally, this is what will ensure that your posts are seen by your target audience. If people are interested in what you are offering, there is a guarantee that they will follow you or take action by purchasing your products.

Popular Social Media Automation Tools

SendinBlue

Usually, marketers compete to reach a wide audience through their marketing campaigns. SendinBlue is a social media automation tool that makes this possible. It is an email marketing tool that can be used by businesses to convert their leads into potential customers and ultimately into loyal clientele. Moreover, the tool gives brands the advantage of nurturing stronger relationships with their customers. Another added advantage of using the automation tool is that it is helpful to marketers who want to automate their Facebook campaigns. The easy-to-use interface makes it a highly recommended tool.

Hootsuite

There is a lot that we have covered on the importance of using a social media calendar. Ideally, with the help of a calendar, you will know what to post and where to post on your social media pages. Hootsuite can make the entire process easy for you. Using this automation tool, you can schedule your posts beforehand on all the social platforms where you have a profile.

An interesting aspect of the tool is that it can be used on a wide array of social media platforms including Facebook, Twitter, LinkedIn, etc. Therefore, you shouldn't have to worry about whether or not it supports a particular social media platform.

What's more, when using the tool, you will be constantly updated on anything that goes on surrounding your brand. For example, you will be notified about brand mentions and comments on your posts. Indeed, this warrants that you engage with your followers and making sure that they don't feel ignored. The best part is that you will benefit from the brand image that you will be creating.

You have probably jumped to the conclusion that this tool is costly. However, it is quite the opposite - it is an inexpensive tool. Therefore, it can be used by business owners who are looking to cut down on their marketing expenses.

BuzzSumo

Marketing on social media is sometimes challenging, more so when you are trying to find fresh content to share. The issue is that you don't want to share content that will drive traffic away from your brand. The good news is that BuzzSumo can help you avoid this. Using certain keywords, you can locate posts that are trending. This should give you an idea of what your clients will be interested to see you post.

You don't have to waste time guessing and trying to figure out what content will appeal to your audience. Using marketing automation tools such as BuzzSumo, the process is made easy for you.

Mention

Just as the name suggests, the Mention automation tool will give you insights concerning your brand mentions. This means that you will not miss out on any social media conversations that surround your brand. The advantage gained here is that you can reap the benefits of these mentions to promote your brand to prospects. Mention will also assist you in carrying out a detailed competitor analysis. Thus, you can adjust your marketing efforts to counter competition from your rivals in the same industry.

Mention can be regarded as a social listening tool. It keeps your ears alert for anything that is related to the products and services that you are dealing with. In line with this, you will have to use keywords to guarantee that you get information on what you want on social media pages.

AgoraPulse

This tool is slightly similar to Hootsuite. However, you get more engagement options when using it to monitor social media activities. There are many things that you can do with this tool, including scheduling posts, analysis, running promotions and contests, collaborate with social media team, etc. You can also use the tool to compare how other rival brands are doing in the market. The tool supports several social media platforms including Facebook, Twitter, Instagram, YouTube, LinkedIn, and Google+.

SocialFlow

Have you ever wondered how big brands use social media effectively to market themselves and fully engage with their audience? Well, with tools such as SocialFlow, it makes it easy to determine the best times to post on social media. This means that you only post when most of your target audience is online and browsing through different social media platforms. Eventually, you will likely experience an increase in your revenues since you will be creating and posting effective campaigns.

Buffer

Just like SocialFlow, Buffer will provide you with reliable insights to help you know when to post. Additionally, the tool is recommended more so to brands that engage in intensive social media marketing. If your brand has profiles on many social networks, then Buffer is what you need to automate your marketing campaign.

Socedo

Another handy social media marketing automation tool is Socedo. This tool stands out from others due to its ability to scan for potential customers that would be interested in your brand. Therefore, with this information, you can make sound decisions on how you will target these people. In addition, the tool also links you to relevant influencers who can help you increase your brand's awareness.

Sprout Social

This automation tool serves you best when you are looking for an all-inclusive one. There are many things that you can automate using this tool. Some of them include tracking mentions, keywords, monitoring competitors, analyzing stats, etc. The best part is that Sprout Social is affordable.

The above list is not an exhaustive list of the best social media automation tools that you can turn to. There are plenty of tools out there, but you should strive to ensure that you go for one that suits your business goals. More importantly, a rule of thumb that you should never forget when using automation tools is that you should still aim to be social.

Social Media Automation Strategy

One major issue with social media automation is that it is easy to get caught up in the process and forget relevance. Automation is not just important to ensure that you boost your engagement with your audience. It also offers you an easier way of integrating an array of social media platforms into your marketing strategy. To ensure that you utilize automation tools effectively, it will be beneficial if you rely on an automation strategy to guide you on your way. Your automation strategy should define a few things which are detailed in the following paragraphs.

Clarify When to Automate

There are many benefits that you will get through automating your social media marketing campaign. As a result, you may easily be tempted to try and automate everything. This is a dilemma that most marketers have to go through. However, it is worth pointing out that you should not try to automate everything. This is because there are some things which should not be automated. Indeed, there is a thin line here and thus you shouldn't blame yourself for trying to find ways of automating everything. Usually, the urge to automate happens to big brands since they lack enough time to go through all their social media pages and engage with their followers. The following are some ideas to help you out when faced with such a dilemma.

Automate Content Curation

Attracting followers to like and share your content will depend on the quality of the posts you share. This makes it worthwhile to invest your time in finding unique content that is worth sharing on social media. You should automate this process since it will have a huge impact on your brand's online presence. The significance of automating this process is that it guarantees that posts are shared at the right time to reach your intended audience. In addition, the idea of automation will give you ample time to research and find great content that resonates with your audience.

Analytics are handy when it comes to knowing what content you should be sharing on your social profiles. However, there is a rule that you can apply to your content sharing process. This rule is known as the 5-3-2 rule. According to this rule, five out of ten content pieces shared should be obtained from third party sources, three of them should be your own creation, and two should be personal that helps to humanize your brand.[34] You should bear in mind that all content posted ought to be relevant to what your target audience would be interested in.

Content obtained from other sources is what is termed as curation. Accordingly, since you will not be creating content here, you should consider automating the process. This gives you more free time to focus on understanding your audience and creating content to their heart's content.

Automate Your RSS Feeds

Running a successful business website demands that you should always keep it updated with informative and engaging content. Undeniably, you will also want to share your posts. As such, this is a process that you can automate to ensure that all your new posts are updated on your social media business pages.

---

[34] "Social Media and the 5:3:2 Rule - LinkedIn." 4 Sep. 2018, https://www.linkedin.com/pulse/social-media-532-rule-stephanie-waide. Accessed 7 Aug. 2019.

Automating saves you time. You don't have to worry about the next time that you should post content on your website.

Automate Non-Pressing Social Media Posts

Of course, there are certain posts which will not be as demanding and therefore you can consider automating when to post them. For example, if you will be posting quotes or sharing other people's thoughts, these are non-urgent posts which should be automated.

Never Automate Customer Interactions

Enough on what you should automate. You should have an idea of what should not be automated in your social media marketing strategy. If are you thinking of automating customer interactions to save you time you should expect negative responses from your clients. Today, people can easily differentiate between authentic responses and automated responses. For that reason, this is a terrible mistake that you could fall for.

There are brands which might think that simple automation such as responding with a simple 'thanks' will not cause any harm. The reality is that it will have a negative impact on the relationship that you build with your audience. Your followers will not value your responses as they are vague.

Never Automate Problem Solving Solutions

Mistakes are a common thing in any business. You can't expect every customer to love your product/service. There are a few individuals who will complain about your product or service on social media. The last thing that you should do is to automate how you help your followers to solve their problems. This puts your business in a negative light. Robotic responses will only make things worse and it could tarnish your business image if these posts are widely shared.

Find a Way of Staying Connected

Sure, you will be looking to automate several aspects of your social media campaign. Nevertheless, you should work to find a way to stay connected. This is an effective way of making sure that you don't miss out on conversations which surround your brand or industry of operation. Luckily, there is an easier way to achieve this. Tracking mentions, for example, will help you stay on track with what people are saying on social media pages. Additionally, you should remember to turn on important notifications depending on the automation tools you will be using.

Chapter 9 - Measuring the ROI of Your Social Media Campaigns

From time to time, you will want to find out whether your social media marketing campaign is getting you the results that you anticipated or not. Certainly, you can't argue that your marketing campaign is successful without proper evaluation. It is imperative that to prove to stakeholders that your investment in social media is paying off. This, therefore, makes it important to measure your return on investment (ROI). This chapter takes a look into why measuring ROI is important and how you can successfully do so.

The value that you generate from your marketing efforts on social media can be measured through the use of ROI. This is a common metric used by marketers to gauge how well they are doing with regard to their marketing campaign. So, why should you measure the ROI of your social media campaigns?

There are several reasons why measuring ROI in any social media marketing campaign is essential. One of the most important reasons is the fact that it shows the value gained from using social media as a marketing channel. In addition, through the metrics that are used in ROI measurements, marketers get to prove that marketing on social media is indeed effective. Additionally, it also helps to indicate the specific marketing tactics which are generating admirable results. At the same time, marketers can use insights to determine marketing efforts that are not yielding good results.

Judging from the above reasons, you can conclude that ROI matters a great deal in your social media marketing campaign. But, the question that you might be asking yourself is, "How do you do it?" Well, here is an outline of what you could do.

Define Your Social Media Objectives

Most people will want to jump into the conclusion that your ROI tells you a lot about how much money you are making from your social media campaigns. The truth is that not all brands use their social media pages to boost their revenues. Some use them to increase their brand's awareness whereas others use social media to increase their engagement with their audience. In addition, there are those who use social platforms as an ideal channel to offer customer service.

The point here is that there are many things that social media can help brands to achieve. For that reason, when measuring your return on investment, you should start by defining your objectives. The significance of doing this is that it gives you an idea of how much you are ready to spend on social media.

Set Practical Goals

Next, you should consider setting practical goals. Goals help to tell you more about how you will be using social media to achieve set objectives. Setting SMART goals here is very important. Say your social media objective is to increase your brand's awareness, a well-structured goal will take the form of: 'Increase brand's social share by 10% in three months.'

Track Performance Metrics

After clarifying your goals and objectives, you will want to find out whether you are achieving these goals and objectives or not. This is where performance metrics come in. There are several metrics that you will have to track and analyze including likes, shares, reach, traffic, engagement, revenue generated, and so on. More about these metrics will be discussed later in this section.

Know Your Social Media Spending

As part of ensuring that you accurately determine your ROI, you should pause and go over the amount you are spending on different social media platforms. In this regard, you will want to measure your returns against several aspects including:

- Cost of Social Channels

Contingent on the social media networks that you will be using, you should strive to find out how much you are getting out of your investment. This applies to situations where the social media platform you use has to be paid for.

- Social Ad Spending

You should also measure your returns against the amount of money you are spending on ads either on Facebook, Twitter, Instagram, etc. The good news is that this is a straightforward process since there are tools which will help you in carrying out the analysis.

- Content Creation

Did you spend money on content creation? If so, how much did you spend? It is important that you include your content creation expenses to make sure that you are getting accurate results on your ROI.

Now that you understand the importance of measuring ROI, let's take a closer look at some of the things that you will be measuring.

Awareness Metrics

Awareness metrics will tell you a lot about the audience that is aware of your brand. Some of the specific metrics that you will be tracking here are as described.

Brand Awareness

This metric illuminates the attention that your brand gets on social media during a specified period. There are several metrics that will help you evaluate your brand awareness including shares, mentions, impressions, and links.

Audience Growth Rate

This metric measures how fast your audience is growing on social media. Essentially, it defines how fast your brand is attracting followers.

Post Reach

This metric will tell you more about the number of people who saw your social media post since it went live.

Potential Reach

Unlike post reach, potential reach tells you the number of individuals who would have seen your post at a certain period. This metric is essential since it helps marketers to continuously expand their audience. Therefore, by measuring potential reach, a marketer can gauge their progress.

Social Share of Voice

When tracking mentions, you will also want to know whether there are more people talking about your brand compared to your rivals. To measure this, the social share of voice metric will help you. It is a competitive analysis of how visible your brand is on social platforms.

Engagement Metrics

Metrics here will tell you more about how your brand interacts with your prospects and customers on social media. Below are some of the metrics that will help you measure social media engagement.

Likes and Shares

The number of likes and shares that you get on your social media page will show you how people are interacting with your posts. It is quite simple to track these metrics since the number of likes or shares is displayed on the social platform that you will be using. When using YouTube, for instance, likes are displayed under the video posted on the platform. The same case applies to Facebook and Twitter.

Audience Growth

It is also imperative that you keep track of how your audience is growing within a specified timeframe. The audience growth metric shows you the rate of your audience growth in a month. By utilizing the insights that you will be getting here, you can increase the number of posts if you notice that there are many people who like what you share. Similarly, if there is a decline in your audience growth, this can be seen as a red flag explaining that your target audience is not impressed with your posts.

Followers

An interesting thing about marketing on social media is that you will only be followed if you follow other people. Therefore, you should look for influencers who could be interested in the products that you are offering. In addition, following some of your customers will also help in getting the word out there about your brand.

It is vital that you find a balance between the number of people that you follow and those that follow your brand. Remember that having many followers doesn't mean that you have an added advantage over your rivals. Quality is more important than quantity. Therefore, it is better to have a few followers who will find your content relevant, rather than having thousands of followers who are rarely moved by your posts.

Clicks Per Post

Businesses will want to share blog posts on their social media pages. The links shared on social media can be tracked to determine the number of clicks people have made to reach the business website. More clicks will indicate that people are interested in what you share. Content is what motivates them to click and follow your brand.

Conversion Metrics

The main reason for posting on social media is that you want to get more conversions. A high number of conversions shows that your social media engagement is highly effective. Key metrics in this category include:

Conversion Rate

A high conversion rate will indicate that your social media campaign is effective. It shows the rate at which your audience are taking the desired actions on your posts. For instance, after viewing your social media ad, they went ahead and purchased a product from you.

Click-Through Rate

The number of times your audience click on your call to action links is measured using the click-through-rate metric. This metric takes your audience to other pages where they can view more content. A high click-through-rate shows that your content is quite compelling.

Bounce Rate

This refers to the percentage of individuals who click on a link on your social media posts, but then quickly leave. A high bounce rate will indicate that you are targeting the wrong audience. Conversely, a low bounce rate will imply that your content resonates with your followers.

Customer Metrics

These are metrics which will provide you with the information you need on how your target audience perceives your brand. Some of the metrics to track here include:

Customer Testimonials

Simply put, these are comments or reviews that talk about a particular brand. It goes without saying that good testimonials will demonstrate that people love your brand. Moreover, if there are several recommendations for your brand, it shows that people are happy with your products/services. If you are looking for more testimonials regarding your brand, you should ask your audience to leave a review behind. When doing this, you should never make the mistake of rewarding the people who leave behind testimonials. Some of your followers will end up concluding that your brand lacks credibility.

Customer Satisfaction Score

The level of satisfaction that customers get from your brand is measured using the customer satisfaction score. To track this metric, you have to create a survey on your social media page to ask customers about how they rate your service provision. Certainly, you must have come across a survey asking you to rate the level of customer satisfaction you gained by depending on a particular brand. The advantage of using this metric is that it is easy to understand and incorporate into your social media marketing campaign. People find it easy to fill out the survey since it doesn't take a lot of time.

Tips to Improve Your Social Media ROI

Besides measuring your social media returns on investment, you should also learn how you can improve ROI. There are several considerations that you should bear in mind here.

You Only Improve What You Measure

Despite the fact that there are numerous businesses which use social media to market their brands, few of them get good ROI. This occurs because most businesses fail to understand the importance of measuring their return on investment. Successful social media marketing is not just about posting content on social media and engaging with your followers. You have to gauge whether you are progressing or not.

When businesses fail to measure their ROI, it means that they are unlikely to improve in their marketing campaigns. Perhaps this is one of the main reasons why brands find themselves struggling to penetrate the noise on social media and reach their intended audience. Therefore, before you think about improving your social media marketing campaign, you should start by measuring your ROI more often.

Understand Who is Engaging with Your Content

Your social media ROI can be improved greatly if you invested time in getting to know the people who interact with your content. Knowing your audience helps you to determine the best metrics to measure your performance.

Define Relevant Metrics

The last thing that you should do is to use particular metrics just because your competitors are using them. This will only mislead you as you will end up measuring statistics which are not relevant to your business. For that reason, you ought to take a step back and evaluate the metrics that work for you. The best way of doing this is by choosing metrics which are in line with your set goals.

Post Frequently

Regular posts are more effective compared to infrequent posts from brands. There is a good chance that customers will want to follow a brand that engages with them more often. When striving to capture your audience's attention by posting regularly, you should make sure that you deliver the right content to them. More importantly, posting at the right time will make a huge difference as it will guarantee that your posts can be seen by your target market.

Choose Ideal Social Media Channels

Choosing the right social media channels to reach your audience is something that should be prioritized above anything else. This is where your audience spends most of their time. Therefore, it is crucial that you make the right decision regarding the platforms that you will be using to post your ads. Posting your social media ads on the wrong platform will only render your marketing campaign ineffective. This is because no one will see what you are posting.

Your first step in your marketing campaign should be to understand your audience. This includes knowing the social media platforms that they use. Targeting them in the right places will boost your chances of improving your ROI.

Create Quality Content

Creating and sharing quality content will also have a positive impact on how people engage with your brand on social media. Your customers expect your content to entertain and educate them. Don't focus too much on selling your brand. Social media requires that you bring in the social aspect of your marketing campaign. As such, humanize your brand by showing people that you can interact with them on a personal level. In the end, they will not hesitate to recommend your brand to their friends on social media.

Motivate Your Social Media Team

Your social media team will greatly influence the success or failure of your social media campaign. If you keep your team motivated, they will work diligently to accomplish your marketing goals and objectives. Motivation here can come in the form of showing your team that you are working with them rather than pushing them around. If possible, ensure that you train them regularly on vital social media marketing tactics that they should implement.

Push for User Engagement

There is no greater feeling than making your audience feel like they are valued. Surprisingly, this is easily achieved by engaging with them. Brands often ignore their customers and give excuses like they lack time to reply to all their customers' comments or complaints. User engagement is key to winning over the hearts of your customers. Therefore, you should think about hiring a team that will specifically work to make sure that your followers are paid attention to.

Always Experiment

Thriving in your social media marketing campaign also calls for experimentation. You have the freedom of trying out different marketing strategies and finding out whether they are effective. You can also experiment by changing your brand's voice and gauging how people respond to the adjustments. It is from such experiments that you can gain a unique marketing strategy that guarantees you accomplish your marketing goals within a short period of time.

Use Real-Time Apps

Customers will fancy the idea of using your social media business app to gain a better engagement experience. This is because there are more customizable engagement options when using your social media business app. Accordingly, you should consider the idea of developing apps which can help bring together people who are not only interested in your brand but those who are looking to connect with your followers.

The bottom line is that measuring your social media marketing ROI ascertains that you know the direction that your social media campaign is taking. Ideally, it is the best way of knowing that you are not operating blindly as you promote your products and services on social media.

Final Thoughts

The introduction of the internet has indeed brought about numerous changes in how people do business. Businesses have taken advantage of the internet to market their brands on social media pages such as Facebook, Twitter, Instagram, YouTube, and Snapchat. The good news is that marketing brands on these social pages are paying off. This is because there are millions of people who have accounts on these platforms. Accordingly, it provides businesses with an opportunity to interact with their audience without spending a lot on their marketing campaigns. If you haven't considered marketing your brand on social media, then you are losing out. The mere fact that you have thought about promoting your brand on these social networks shows that you must have noticed how your competitors are using these channels to their advantage.

The truth is that it is worth investing in social media marketing if you aspire to grow your business. Bearing in mind that there are millions of people on different social accounts, this means that promoting your brand here will help you reach many people. The benefit gained here is that there will be an increase in the demand for your products and services. Demand for your products and services will be given a huge boost since people are always on the lookout for brands that solve the problems they are facing. As such, if you present your brand in a way that captures your target market's attention, then there is a good chance that they will want more of your product.

You should also recognize and acknowledge the fact that people who visit social media pages are accustomed to the idea of social buying. Today, purchasing products using social media is increasingly common. In fact, people consider this the best way to get reliable information on what they should buy. Having said this, running a successful business, therefore, demands that you should also compete to engage in social selling. People who are on Facebook, Twitter, Instagram, and the likes, are the same individuals who expect your brand to offer them practical solutions to their everyday requirements. So, social media marketing offers you the advantage of trying out social selling as a way of reaching your audience.

That's not all, promoting your brand on social media aids in boosting your SEO rankings on different search engines such as Google, Bing, Yahoo, etc. Social media accounts are not only used for engagement purposes. People have relied on these accounts to search for information. The more people search for your brand using these channels, the better your SEO rankings. Ultimately, this will offer you an added advantage of increasing your follower count.

In order to get the best out of your social media campaign, you will have to develop a marketing strategy. Promoting your brand on social media doesn't just entail sharing content with your followers. There is more to social media marketing than just creating and sharing posts. An integral part of your strategy requires that you should understand your audience. Without a doubt, if you are looking to post content that resonates with your target audience, it is imperative that you understand who they are. In addition, you should find out more about where they socialize over the internet. Do they use Facebook more compared to Instagram? What types of videos do they love seeing? What type of content entertains them? These are some of the things that you should find out about your audience before thinking about posting ads.

Your social media marketing goals will also be a determining factor on what you will be sharing to these social media accounts. For instance, if you are on social media to increase awareness, there are specific marketing strategies that you will adopt. In this case, your marketing goals will be to try and ensure people can recall the name of your brand or to differentiate your brand logo with rival companies.

Content is king when it comes to social media marketing. People will share your content if they feel that your content is informative, entertaining, or helpful. Additionally, social media users will want to be associated with brands which share engaging content. For that reason, you can't share just anything and expect people to like, share, or retweet your content. To guarantee that you succeed in creating engaging content, it is imperative that you always think about your target audience. These are the people who will be consuming your products. As such, you ought to mull over their tastes and preferences before posting anything.

Still on content, your followers will want to share your content if they get regular updates on your social media business page. This means that you should focus on maintaining consistency on how you post content. Posting one day and disappearing for weeks is not the best way of showing your audience that you are a reliable brand. For that reason, it is prudent that you consider the recommended posting schedule which has been detailed for you in this manual.

Most entrepreneurs who are new to social media marketing will assume that for them to attract a large following, they should have many social media business profiles. This is not the case - there are big brands who focus their marketing efforts on a few social media pages and have a huge following. Marketing on social media is centered around the idea of quality over quantity. Therefore, when choosing the right social channel to engage with your followers, you should only go for the few that help you meet your business goals.

In conjunction with what has been said above, you should choose an ideal social media platform based on your target audience. You should take time to ask yourself whether your customers are on the social media channel that you plan to use. For instance, statistics show that there are more women than men on Pinterest. What does this tell you? If you are targeting women with your product, then you should consider making a business account on Pinterest. Moreover, if your target market is composed of young people, the best platform to reach them will be Instagram. The point here is that you don't have to have social media accounts on all platform for you to be successful in your marketing campaign. Knowing your business goals and prioritizing the social channels that help you achieve these goals will help you settle for the most suitable ones. Therefore, don't fall for the hype that having an account on the most popular social media platforms will guarantee that you attract a large following.

Another crucial aspect of social media marketing that needs to be stressed is the importance of having a social media calendar. Keeping up with marketing activities on social media is not an easy job. If you have an account on multiple channels, there is a chance that you will find it strenuous to post on these pages. In fact, there are times when you will forget to post. This will affect your marketing campaign since your posts might not reach your intended audience.

With the help of a social media calendar, you will find it easy to maintain a consistent posting schedule. This will be of great importance in making sure that your content reaches your intended audience. You should bear in mind that posting at the right time every day increases the likelihood of growing a large audience. More importantly, it saves you from the common error of posting the wrong content on the wrong platforms. Indeed, mistakes happen. If you are in a hurry to post content, then rest assured that you could end up requesting your Facebook audience to retweet your content instead of asking them to like and share.

Of course, you should also think about offering your followers with a seamless experience when engaging with them within any marketing channel that you opt to use. Technology has brought about diversity in the way businesses can connect with their clients. Customers are also aware of this fact and are always on the lookout for brands which can provide them with a seamless shopping experience. Think about it this way, customers will not want to feel as though they are being pushed from one device to the other or from one social application to the other. So, brands should strive to offer customers a way of moving from one social platform to the other without being inconvenienced.

Bearing in mind that there is a lot that you will want to handle in your social media, you ought to consider automating certain activities. Automation will save you time. You will find some free time to focus on more important activities such as creating high-quality content. Automating doesn't mean that you should robotize everything. You should understand that not everything can be automated. Knowing what to automate and what to do manually will ensure that you don't make mistakes that will tarnish your brand's reputation. You can automate content curation, but you can't automate customer interactions. People expect to engage with your brand on a personalized level. They expect to see your brand's personality through the way in which you engage with them. Therefore, automating your interactions will only discourage them from following you or sharing your content.

On a final note, you should always remember to measure the ROI of your social media campaigns. You can't operate blindly without knowing whether you are making progress or not. Measuring your ROI gives you the insight that you require to make necessary changes in areas where your marketing efforts are not paying off. In a way, it helps to illuminate the right path that you should be taking to guarantee that you maximize your ROI. Your return on investment doesn't necessarily mean that you should focus solely on increasing your revenue. Rather, you should look at the bigger picture. Social media marketing can help you boost your brand's recognition. It can also increase your followers if people are interested in what you share. So, it's not all about increased revenue for you to conclude that your marketing efforts are working.

Luckily, there are several recommended tools which you can use to measure your social media ROI. Some of these tools are free whereas others require you to sign up for premium versions. The important thing that you should think about is whether the tools suit your business demands or not. All in all, marketing your brand on social media will get you the results that you want.

Utilize the tips which have been discussed in this guide and remember you don't have to be perfect; you only need to stick to recommended strategies of promoting your brand on social media.

Good luck!

References

126 Amazing Social Media Statistics and Facts. (n.d.). Retrieved from https://www.brandwatch.com/blog/amazing-social-media-statistics-and-facts/

17 Instagram stats marketers need to know for 2019. (2019, April 22). Retrieved from https://sproutsocial.com/insights/instagram-stats/

21+ Incredible Instagram Stories Stats to Know in 2019. (2019, May 9). Retrieved from https://99firms.com/blog/instagram-stories-statistics/

77 Online Shopping Statistics for 2019. (2019, June 7). Retrieved from https://hostingfacts.com/online-shopping-statistics/

The 80/20 rule for social media and ideas to help you achieve it. (2018). Retrieved from https://www.shakeitupcreative.com/2018/03/05/the-80-20-rule-for-social-media-and-ideas-to-help-you-achieve-it/

85 Content Marketing Statistics To Make You A Marketing Genius. (2019, January 7). Retrieved from https://optinmonster.com/content-marketing-statistics/

Agius, A. (n.d.). 12 Examples of Brands With Brilliant Omni-Channel Experiences. Retrieved from https://blog.hubspot.com/service/omni-channel-experience

Benefits of social media marketing worldwide 2019. (n.d.). Retrieved from https://www.statista.com/statistics/188447/influence-of-global-social-media-marketing-usage-on-businesses/

CoSchedule. (n.d.). How Often To Post On Social Media According To 14 Studies. Retrieved from https://coschedule.com/blog/how-often-to-post-on-social-media/

Demographics of Social Media Users and Adoption in the United States. (n.d.). Retrieved from https://www.pewinternet.org/fact-sheet/social-media/

Facebook users worldwide 2019. (n.d.). Retrieved from https://www.statista.com/statistics/264810/number-of-monthly-active-facebook-users-worldwide/

Facebook: global daily active users 2019. (n.d.). Retrieved from https://www.statista.com/statistics/346167/facebook-global-dau/

Global digital population 2019. (n.d.). Retrieved from https://www.statista.com/statistics/617136/digital-population-worldwide/

Lucy Handley, special to CNBC. (2017, February 16). Sixty-five percent of people skip online video ads. Here's what to do about it. Retrieved from https://www.cnbc.com/2017/02/16/sixty-five-percent-of-people-skip-online-video-ads-heres-what-to-do.html

Mohsin, M. (2019, August 2). 10 Video Marketing Statistics for 2019 [Infographic]. Retrieved from https://www.oberlo.com/blog/video-marketing-statistics

The Must-Have Social Media Content Strategy for Your Brand. (2017, November 29). Retrieved from https://sproutsocial.com/insights/social-media-content-strategy/

Social Media and the 5:3:2 Rule. (n.d.). Retrieved from https://www.linkedin.com/pulse/social-media-532-rule-stephanie-waide

Social Media Platforms and Demographics. (n.d.). Retrieved from https://info.lse.ac.uk/staff/divisions/communications-division/digital-communications-team/assets/documents/guides/A-Guide-To-Social-Media-Platforms-and-Demographics.pdf

Social Media Use 2018: Demographics and Statistics. (2019, April 17). Retrieved from https://www.pewinternet.org/2018/03/01/social-media-use-in-2018/

Social Media Use 2018: Demographics and Statistics. (2019, April 17). Retrieved from https://www.pewinternet.org/2018/03/01/social-media-use-in-2018/

U.S. Pinterest user distribution by gender 2019. (n.d.). Retrieved from https://www.statista.com/statistics/408229/us-pinterest-user-gender/

Use of different online platforms by demographic groups. (n.d.). Retrieved from https://www.pewinternet.org/2018/03/01/social-media-use-in-2018/pi_2018-03-01_social-media_a-01/

What Is Influencer Marketing And How Can Marketers Use It. (n.d.). Retrieved from https://www.forbes.com/sites/forbescommunicationscouncil/2017/11/14/what-is-influencer-marketing-and-how-can-marketers-use-it-effectively/

Yeung, K. (2016, September 30). Facebook: 60 million businesses have Pages, 4 million actively advertise. Retrieved from https://venturebeat.com/2016/09/27/facebook-60-million-businesses-have-pages-4-million-actively-advertise/

Made in the
USA
Monee, IL